FIRE
ON THE
ALTAR

FIRE
ON THE
ALTAR

WINNING *the* BATTLE
THROUGH UNCONDITIONAL SURRENDER

PERRY FRED STONE, SR.

COPPER SCROLL
PUBLISHING

FIRE ON THE ALTAR

Published by CopperScroll Publishers
Post Office Box 5298
Cleveland, Tennessee 37311
e-mail: copperscroll@charter.net

Unless otherwise noted, all Scripture quotations are from the New King James Version of the Bible. Copyright © 1982 by Thomas Nelson, Inc. Used by permission. All rights reserved.

Scripture quotations marked KJV are from the King James Version of the Bible.

Cover Design by Michael Dutton, www.atomicpress.com

Printed by Modern Way Printing and Fulfillment
8817 Production Lane, Ooltewah, TN 37363
www.modernwayco.com

ISBN 1-934213-07-1

First Edition

Printed in the United States of America

Contents

Section 3: We Need the Fire

Foreword

Joshua was over eighty years old when he led the younger Israelites, under forty years of age and born in the wilderness, into the Promised Land. Joshua and these wilderness children saw the great works of the Lord. However, a generation arose later that forgot the Lord and the miracles he did for Israel. We are told of this in two Bible verses that have always troubled my spirit:

"So the people served the LORD all the days of Joshua, and all the days of the elders who outlived Joshua, who had seen all the great works of the LORD, which he had done for Israel" (Judges 2:7).

"When all that generation had been gathered to their fathers, another generation arose after them who did not know the LORD nor the work which he had done for Israel" (Judges 2:10).

This seems to describe our generation, which is spiritually lacking in many areas. Most local churches never experience the manifestations of the Holy Spirit. The younger generation has little, if any, experience in the operation of the nine gifts of the Spirit. I humbly say that I have seen all nine gifts operate in the ministry of my father, Fred Stone.

My father was converted to the Lord during a revival that lasted forty-two months. His desire for prayer, fasting, and intimacy with God thrust him into a spiritual dimension that few ministers experience. From the beginning, he operated in the gifts of the Spirit. Amazing miracles followed his ministry. Even as a child, I remember seeing the Holy Spirit speak to Dad when he would call people out from the congregation and reveal things that nobody knew except that person and the Lord.

I have seen him pray in the Spirit and watched as foreigners would say, "You just prayed for me in my native language!" Dad had no formal education in foreign languages, but he was exercising the gift of different tongues. The Lord often gave him advance warnings of trouble for church members, our family, and even the nations of the world. His humility shows when I discuss some of the examples with other people. He prefers not to speak about some things publicly, especially when leaders from government organizations call him to discuss an accurate vision the Lord gave him.

This book is not just a testimony about a miraculous revival. It is a resource to inspire the next generation. Dad will reveal secrets of intercessory prayer and how the gifts of the Spirit operate in the believer's life. God has not changed and neither has His Holy Spirit! May this book inspire you to draw closer to God and seek His presence in your life. May this generation say, "We remember the Lord, and we have seen His great works in our lifetime." I am honored that this man is my father and that he has impacted my life. May these words impact yours!

Keep the fire burning on the altar!
Perry Stone, Jr.

Preface

Too many Christians are confused. Confused about what to believe, whom to believe, and why to believe. We live in an age when the true gospel message has been watered down or even discarded. And sadly, the message of the Holy Spirit with His power and authority has been replaced with a message of prosperity and endless blessings. In these days of tolerance, we want to make sure we don't offend anybody. In these days of enlightenment and modern technology, we think we can do everything without Him.

Isn't that just like the enemy to hide the power of the Holy Spirit from the church? After all, the power and authority of the Holy Spirit will defeat the enemy and bring glory to God. When you are easy bait for Satan, he can destroy you, your family, your church, and your nation. The enemy knows that a powerless and defeated Christian cannot be used by God.

Every day we need to put on the armor of God to battle the enemy. But make no mistake: We also need the power and authority of the Holy Spirit. In Judges 6:34, when the Spirit of the Lord came upon Gideon, that verse in Hebrew literally means that the Spirit of the Lord clothed

Himself in Gideon. He *took possession* of Gideon. We need to let the Holy Spirit of the Lord take possession of us every single day.

Jesus told His disciples, *"You shall receive power when the Holy Spirit has come upon you."* They received power to witness, to spread the gospel, to perform miracles, and to battle the demons of hell that Jesus defeated on the cross. They received power that glorified the Almighty God.

Through the infilling and the gifts of the Holy Spirit, you also can become a vessel that is full of power and authority from on High. You can bring glory and honor to God, and encouragement and deliverance to your family, your church, and even the nations. In these last days, we need to bring God's power out of hiding and reveal to the world His awesome and mighty works. He wants to pour out His Spirit upon all flesh. He wants to empower us to glorify His name through miracles. He wants us to pray for the sick so they can be healed. He wants to give us divine protection. And He wants to reveal to us the trouble that is on the horizon. How can we say no to that?

In this book, I tell the story of the early years of my life in the coal mining town of Bartley, West Virginia. I tell how the Lord saved me as a teenager, filled me with the Holy Spirit, called me into ministry, and introduced me to the astonishing power, authority, and miracles that come with the gifts of the Spirit. I explain each gift of the Holy Spirit and give modern-day examples of how the gifts have operated in my own life and ministry. And finally, there are answers to questions often asked by people who are unfamiliar with the Holy Spirit, followed by scripture references for personal or group study.

Where would I be today if the Lord hadn't touched my life as a teenager and placed me in a church that operated in the fullness of the

Holy Spirit? I might have spent time in prison; maybe I would not be alive today. But I thank God that He saw something in a skinny, black-haired boy in the coalfields of West Virginia and chose me to live my life in service to Him. The love and blessings of God, and the power of the Holy Spirit, are just as real to me today as they were over fifty years ago in that little church in Flat Top, West Virginia. I still feel the great love of God in my soul. He is real—all the time. The Holy Spirit is real—all the time.

My prayer is that, by the time you finish reading this book, you will have a steadfast desire for more of God. He is the same yesterday, today, and forever. What He did two thousand years ago, He will still do today.

May God richly bless you and your family. I pray that He, through the power of His Holy Spirit, will create a spiritual hunger in your life to draw closer to Him. I pray that He will work mightily through every child of God who is hungry for more of Him.

SECTION ONE
Appalachian Fire

"The fear of the LORD prolongs days,
but the years of the wicked will be shortened.
The hope of the righteous will be gladness,
but the expectation of the wicked will perish.
The way of the LORD is strength for the upright,
but destruction will come to the workers of iniquity."

———————————

PROVERBS 10:27–29

"As righteousness leads to life,
so he who pursues evil pursues it to his own death."

———————————

PROVERBS 11:19

CHAPTER 1

Life in a Coal Mining Town

Nestled in a valley between the lush green mountains of southern West Virginia sits the small, coal mining town of Bartley. I always said that God must have loved that part of the world because, when He made it, He kept piling it on. Neighboring towns of Iaeger, English, War, and Bradshaw were so close to Eastern Kentucky and Southwestern Virginia that they might have hunted the same deer. Deep inside these Appalachian Mountains are the mines that once were characterized as West Virginia's billion dollar coalfields. Those words were even written on public transportation vehicles.

The land was rich and fertile, producing almost anything that was edible. Even the smallest farms had orchards, with trees that were loaded in season with apples and pears. Chestnuts and black walnuts were plentiful. Every year, the men planted acres of corn, beans, peas, potatoes, and any other vegetable that could be stored in a cellar or canned in jars to provide food through the winter and spring. Families raised chickens, pigs, and cows; but most of the meat came from the men who hunted whatever animal they could shoot and bring home for dinner. We were always blessed with plenty of good food.

Most of the people in these rural coal mining settlements were poor folks who had few material possessions. They typically owned the barest necessities—a few items of clothing for each family member; just enough furniture for sitting and sleeping; basic dinnerware and cooking utensils; and of course, shotguns.

Families were large, often with ten or more children. My mother, Nalva Verda Glaca Dunford, had four brothers and four sisters. Like many children in those days, she was named after three of her relatives. She wasn't fond of her names, so she preferred to be called Nalvie. It seemed that every mother birthed at least one child who died as an infant or a toddler. My mother would eventually give birth to twelve children, ten of whom survived to adulthood.

People identified their neighborhood by the name of their hollow (or "holler" if you were a local). A hollow was a rugged cove with farms and log houses situated in a valley between the mountains. Since there was no indoor plumbing, homes were built close to a spring for collecting water, and there was nearly always a creek running through the woods. My family lived in Johnny Cake Hollow.

Mining was the primary industry, so most of the men worked in the coal mines. Those were the days before modern mining equipment, and the work was even more grueling and hazardous than it is today. Life in these mining communities was challenging enough without being marred by sorrow, violence, and tragedy. But that, too, was as much a part of life as walking to work every day.

My maternal grandfather, Sam Dunford, bore a striking resemblance to Samuel Clemmons, the author who penned under the name Mark Twain. Sam Dunford was one of the few men who did not work in the mines; instead, he was a farmer and a trader. He and his sons were talented musicians who gathered on the weekends to play bluegrass music on banjos and violins. Unfortunately, Sam also made and sold moonshine whiskey to people who came from miles around to buy it. He and his sons often partook of the work of their hands, which meant they were frequently drunk, ill-tempered, and combative.

In most households, you could find a large family Bible—the kind that was sold by traveling salesmen who peddled them door to door. These Bibles had pages in the front to log the names and birthdates of each family member. And since the Bible stayed on the shelf most of the time, it also served as a safe place to story family photos and important documents.

The Dunford family owned one of those Bibles and, like most, it collected dust. But sometimes Sam Dunford would gather the children, take the family Bible off the shelf, and read a few passages. Outside of those rare occasions of scripture reading, God's name was spoken only as a curse word.

Every family owned several guns, and they all knew how to shoot them. Since hunting was the primary method for putting meat on the table, every boy who was big enough to carry a gun could shoot before he could add and subtract. With enough practice, they could hit nearly any target with bulls-eye accuracy. But sometimes they used their skill to take the law into their own hands. The consequences were often tragic.

One of the Dunford boys was named Hershel—a handsome young man with the looks of a movie star. He attended school with a boy named Earl Ray who had a reputation for being a bully. He often beat up other boys, and Hershel was one of his victims. He would whip Hershel on the way to or from school, and often in front of other classmates. It embarrassed Hershel; so after a fight one day, he decided to get revenge.

Since the family needed all the meat they could kill, Hershel skipped school one day and told his mother that he wanted to shoot a deer that he had seen in a nearby hollow. She gave him shells and a rifle that was usually kept under lock and key, and he left.

With the rifle in hand, Hershel sat behind some trees and waited patiently for Earl Ray to come home from school. As the boy walked home alone, Hershel raised the rifle and fired one shot at him. He missed, and Earl Ray jumped behind the fallen trunk of a huge chestnut tree. When he raised his head to see where the shot had come from, Hershel shot him right between the eyes and killed him.

Hershel went home and told his mother that he had shot at the deer, but missed. Earl Ray was found dead a short time later, and Hershel was arrested and charged with murder. He was sent to prison in Moundsville, West Virginia and that is where he died. The prison shipped his body back to English, West Virginia on a train, and the family said that his body was covered with bruises. They were never able to find out what happened to him in prison, but they were certain that someone had beaten him to death. Nothing was ever done about it, and prison officials denied that such beating ever occurred.

That same dark curse of tragedy, adversity, and misery would follow the Dunford clan for years to come.

My mother, Nalvie, was a young, attractive, dark-haired girl who married a man from Council, Virginia named Arthur Ball. Within the first few years of their marriage, Nalvie and Arthur had two children, Lola Mae and Morgan. The four of them lived with Nalvie's parents in Johnny Cake Hollow.

The two children were still very small—Morgan was just an infant—when Arthur took the dog and left the house one day to go hunting. Before long, the dog came back home alone. That was unusual, but soon the dog left again so Nalvie didn't think much of it. But long after Arthur should have been home, there was still no sign of him. Nalvie realized something was wrong. Family and neighbors were sent into the woods to check on him.

About a quarter of a mile from the house, they found his body. He was lying on a pile of tree branches and other brush that had been stacked so that it could be burned later. It appeared that Arthur had stood on this brush pile to shoot something and had slipped, falling forward on his face. As he fell, the gun discharged, hitting him in the chin and blowing away an eye and much of the front of his face.

The weather was cool, and he had been wearing a jacket, a wool shirt, and an undershirt. When the men found him, his clothes were beaten to shreds from where he tried to get up but kept falling back down. Apparently it took him a while to die.

The men carried him home, wrapped him in a quilt, and left him lying on the front porch while they built a casket. Those who heard about the accident came to the home to pay their respects, all the while unrolling the quilt from Arthur's body to look at him and make comments. There was Nalvie, sobbing and wailing each time someone removed the quilt and exposed his mortal remains. The effect on her emotional well-being would last many years.

Never did she expect to be a young widow with two small children to care for. Shortly after Arthur's accident, Nalvie started drowning her sorrows in liquor, which was plentiful since her father made and sold moonshine.

William Henry Stone and Nalvie Dunford Ball had known each other for years because they lived on adjoining farms. Within two years of Arthur's death, they married and moved into a home that Sam Dunford built in Johnny Cake Hollow. I was born the following year.

———◇———

The weather was snowy and wintry cold when Mom went into labor on February 11, 1933. Dad left home early that morning to walk to Bradshaw, West Virginia to find a doctor who would come to the house and deliver me. Dad trampled seven miles through snow with temperatures below freezing before he found a coal company doctor. In those days, each coal company hired their own doctor, so his first obligation was to the employees of the coal company that hired him. But this doctor agreed to drive Dad back to the house for the delivery.

They both got into the doctor's car; but before they had gone very far, a coal company employee flagged down the car and said that the doctor's services were needed by an employee's wife. Dad got out of the car and trudged through several more miles of snow to Yukon, West Virginia where he found a Dr. Hatfield. They got into the doctor's Model-A Ford and drove to Johnny Cake Hollow. Since it was impossible to drive the car beyond the edge of the hollow, they were met by a neighbor, Grover Hatfield, who was waiting for them on horseback. He brought another horse for the doctor to ride, while Dad followed behind on foot.

The men were about two hundred feet from the house when they passed a woman carrying a bundle under her arm. They didn't know what the woman was carrying until they heard Nalvie, who was standing in the doorway yelling, "Stop that woman! Stop her, she's got the baby!"

It was now late afternoon, and I had been born before Dad returned. This woman—a relative of mom's who had neither married nor had children of her own—had served as a midwife. After the delivery, she decided to keep the baby. Dad and the doctor stopped the woman and tried to take the bundle from her arms as the woman fought them and insisted, "This is my baby! God sent me to this house to get my baby!"

Mom, having just given birth, was in no condition to chase this woman through the cold and the snow. Dad and the doctor arrived just in time to seize me from the woman's arms.

My parents had not chosen a name for me, so Dad named me Perry, after some of his relatives in North Carolina. The doctor said, "I almost froze to death getting here and I might freeze to death before I get back, so I'm giving this baby a name, too. The doctor chose the name Fred, after a Broadway actor of that day named Fred Stone. From that day on, everybody in my family called me Freddie.

I had another close call when I was about two years old. Mom's brother, Rufus Dunford, saved my life that time. But before I tell you my story, I will tell you his.

Around 1931, after suffering with severe headaches and double vision, Rufus was diagnosed with a brain tumor. Even the doctors at Johns Hopkins told him that there was no hope for a recovery and nothing could be done. They said that he would soon be unable to care for himself and, eventually, he would die.

Like the rest of the Dunford men, Rufus did not have a personal relationship with the Lord and was not a praying man. His wife Mamie was an Italian, so she had some knowledge of God because of her Roman Catholic background. She often encouraged Rufus to fast and pray about his situation.

As his condition worsened, Rufus stopped eating. For three days he fasted; then, he decided that it couldn't hurt to take Mamie's advice and pray. He prayed a simple, heartfelt prayer: "If there is a God, and I don't know if there is or not, I don't want to leave Mamie and the kids. If you'll heal me, I promise that I'll live for you for the rest of my life."

Not long after that, he was digging potatoes in the field when the power of God in the form of a whirlwind struck him and knocked him on his back. He started praying, and the more he prayed, the better he felt. Before long, he started quoting the entire sixteenth chapter of the book of Mark, which talks about Jesus being raised from the dead, about the great commission to preach the gospel to every creature, and about signs and wonders following those who believe. Rufus had never in his life even read the book of Mark. In fact, he had a third grade education and could not read very well.

As he lay there, he started speaking in tongues. While he was on the ground praying, speaking in tongues, and quoting scripture that he had never read, the Lord said to him, "I have forgiven you of your sins, I have healed you, I have filled you with the Holy Spirit, and I have given you the gift of divers kinds of tongues. When you get off your back, you will be able to witness to any nationality of men that I put before you."

Mamie looked out the window and saw Rufus lying in the field. She, their daughters Nalvie and Bessie, and Grandma Allie Dunford rushed outside to see what was happening. They heard Rufus speaking loudly in a language they did not understand. Of course they had no idea what was happening because they knew nothing about the baptism of the Holy Spirit. They listened to him for a while and tried to talk to him. But Rufus was not able to respond because he was still under the power of the Holy Spirit.

Grandma Dunford said, "Poor ol' thing. It looks like that tumor has busted on his brain. He's trying to talk to us and he can't." Fearing the worst, one of the women ran to get the men who were working in the fields.

They rushed to the scene; but by the time they arrived, the Spirit of the Lord had lifted off Rufus. He didn't understand what just happened; but as he sat on the ground, he tried to explain it the best he could.

From that moment on, the family saw a dramatic change in Rufus' life. He stopped drinking moonshine and got a job in the mines. He asked Mamie to read the Bible to him, and he started preaching every time the Lord gave him an opportunity. There were many immigrants—German, Polish, Greek, Italian, Romanian, and Hungarian—settling in that part of West Virginia, and they spoke very little broken English. Rufus could walk up to a stranger of any nationality and, through the power of the Holy Spirit, witness to them by speaking perfectly in their language.

The women in the family respected Rufus, but the men laughed and mocked him to his face. As the only man in his family who was a believer—and a Spirit-filled one at that—he endured much persecution from his own relatives. But thankfully, I had an uncle who knew how to pray for the sick, because I was going to need his prayers when I was two years old.

Dad would sometimes buy chestnuts at the company store and cook them, giving each of us children one or two of them. In our yard, we had a tree full of buckeyes, which have a dark, hard shell. I thought these buckeyes were chestnuts, so I ate a few of them.

Buckeyes are poisonous, and in a short time I was deathly sick. I appeared lifeless and my eyes were glassy. Mom was certain I was dying. Dad was working in the mines and Mom had no way to reach him, so she sent somebody to find Rufus.

About two hours later, Rufus showed up at the house. He prayed a powerful, anointed prayer over me, rebuking the poison and commanding that it be harmless and leave my body. He continued to pray powerfully in the Spirit. Within moments of his prayer, I jumped up, pointed to my mouth, and vomited. Almost immediately afterward, I was running around the house and playing with Morgan and Lola. I have no doubt that I received a supernatural touch of God that day. Thank God for at least one family member who knew how to pray!

By today's standards, our family—and most others in that part of the country—would have been considered poor. Our log house had one large room with a fireplace for heat and a potbellied stove for cooking. There were no partitions to divide the room, and of course, no indoor plumbing. Water was carried by bucket from a spring that was about fifty feet from the house. There were only two beds in the tiny house so, in our younger years, the children were all tucked into the same bed at night. If the girls slept at the head of the bed, the boys slept at the foot.

Since we were the first three children in the family and only a few years apart in age, Lola, Morgan and I were always very close. We managed to enjoy ourselves, in spite of the problems and circumstances around us. One Christmas when we were still very young, Uncle Rob Dunford donned a Santa outfit and came to our house. Having no clue that it was Uncle Rob, we children were in awe, thinking for certain that Santa had dropped into our yard straight from the North Pole.

Uncle Rob asked if we had been good enough to get something for Christmas. I kept repeating, "Santa, Morgan's been a good boy. Morgan's been a real good boy. He's not been mean or nothing. Morgan's been good. You've got to bring Morgan something. Morgan's been real good." I don't know if Lola and I had been good, but apparently Morgan had.

Dad cut down a tree from the woods behind our house, and Mom decorated it with homemade decorations. At the top of the tree sat a white angel. As a coal miner, Dad's wages were about forty cents an hour, but every Christmas, he bought each of us an orange, an apple, a banana, and hard candy from the company store. That was a typical Christmas gift, and we were thrilled to get it.

But one thing that did negatively affect us as children was moonshine liquor. Dad always despised being around drunkards and, as far as I know, he never drank alcohol in his life. But he was surrounded by bootleggers and alcoholics who lived a wretched lifestyle because of their addiction to moonshine.

Mom never touched liquor until her first husband, Arthur, was killed in the hunting accident. But after she started drinking, she became an alcoholic and remained one for years. Once she took the first drink, she kept drinking until there was nothing left to drink.

As long as Mom was sober, she was the sweetest person you would ever meet, and she and Dad got along very well. But when she was intoxicated, her personality changed completely. She became mouthy and defiant, just like her father and brothers when they were drunk. That, combined with Dad's temper, caused a lot of strife between the two of them. Mom and Dad had many heated arguments when Mom was drunk.

Sometimes Mom would drink when she visited her family. Other times, her brothers would visit us while Dad was at work and bring their moonshine with them. They all sat in our house and drank moonshine until they were intoxicated, loud, and obnoxious. Mom's brothers knew that Dad despised that kind of lifestyle and would not have permitted such behavior in our home.

Dad raised chickens to feed the family and, after Mom's relatives sat in our house drinking all afternoon, they would ask her to fix chicken and cornbread. Somebody would go to the chicken house and kill one of our chickens, which Mom would cook while the men sat in our house drinking until it was almost time for Dad to come home. I didn't want to be around these drunkards, either, and I remember as a child being glad to hear them say, "Bill will be home soon. I guess we'd better get going." They knew that if Dad came home and found them at our house, he might have grabbed a gun and run them off.

One day Dad came home from work and found that Mom had left Morgan, Lola, and me at home alone while she went to visit her parents. He knew that she had most likely gone there for moonshine, and he was furious. He took off to get her with the three of us following at his heels.

We crossed over a small wooden bridge and walked up the side of the creek next to the Dunford property. We came close enough to the house for Dad to yell for Mom to come outside. There were a couple of drunken men on the porch, and Mom had been drinking as well. Mom crawled through the rail fence and Dad said something to her about leaving the kids at home alone and being up there with those drunken bums. Then he slapped her.

When he did, a distant relative named Jim Dunford—a huge guy, maybe 6'4 and 275 pounds—cursed Dad and left the porch. He crossed the fence and headed toward Dad, but Dad stood his ground. Mom was terrified because she knew there was going to be a confrontation. Dad expected a fistfight, but when Jim got several feet from Dad, he stooped in the creek and picked up a rock in each hand. Dad also picked up a rock in each hand and the two of them stood in the creek, slamming each other with rocks.

Since Dad weighed about 160 pounds, it didn't take long for Jim to overpower him. Jim got Dad on his back in the creek and kept beating him with rocks. The situation was not looking good for Dad.

Grandma Dunford sent my cousin, Darrie Whittaker, to call for his stepfather, Uri Davidson, who was a good friend of Dad's. Uri rushed to the creek, where Dad was now a bloody mess from being beaten up with rocks by a drunken man who was almost twice his size. Uri threw a rifle to the back of Jim's neck and said, "I'll empty every bullet into your head if you hit Bill one more time."

Uri and another man picked Dad up and carried him back to the house. He was beaten so badly that he could not work in the mines for the next two days.

A month later, a sober Jim Dunford came to our house and apologized to Dad for beating him. He gave Dad a pearl-handled knife, perhaps in an effort to make peace. But Jim was an abusive scoundrel when he was drunk, and that might have contributed to his demise. One night he left his job in the coal mines and walked toward home, but he never arrived. The following morning he was found dead—shot twice with a 12-gauge shotgun. The fellow who confessed to the shooting went to prison for several years.

———◇———

Dad had no tolerance for drunkards, but he wasn't aware that his youngest brother, Crockett, also made and sold moonshine. When my brother Morgan was about eight years old, he would sneak into the hills and watch them at their moonshine still. One day he said, "Freddie, let's go up in the holler. I want to show you something."

So Morgan and I went into the hills and he took me straight to the moonshine still. There were a couple of barrels, copper tubing, stacks of wood, and piles of ashes.

Morgan ordered me not to tell anybody. "Uncle Crockett will be in trouble if Dad finds out." I had no idea what Uncle Crockett was doing that might get him in trouble with Dad, but I agreed to keep quiet about it.

By this time, I had another sister named Allie Mary who was two years younger than I was. One day she told me about a jug that Uncle Crockett had in the fodder shock, which was a huge bundle of stripped corn stalks that had been stacked up to dry.

"What's in the jug?" I asked her.

"I don't know what it is, but people come here and bring little bottles in their pockets. Uncle Crockett takes a bottle and opens it up, then pours something out of that jug into their bottles. They give him some money, and Uncle Crockett puts the jug back in the fodder shock."

She and I went to the fodder shock, which was a few hundred yards from our house, and felt around the corn stalks until we found a jug. We lugged it back toward the house until we came to Granddad Stone's barn. Allie Mary and I helped each other into the barn, and we sat facing each other in the doorway as we took the cork out of the jug.

We sniffed the contents and I concluded, "They couldn't drink this stuff. It stinks too bad."

"Yeah, they drink it. I've seen them drink it," she said.

She dared me to take a drink. "I'll take a drink if you go first."

After some hesitation, I took the dare. I raised the jug and took a small sip. It felt like liquid fire going down my throat. She took a sip, and then I took another sip, and we continued this back and forth. We could take only small sips because it felt like we were drinking fire.

We were discussing what the contents in the jug could be when we started to feel dizzy. We jumped down from the barn entrance and I reached over to get the jug, which by that time had started moving—first left and right, then back and forth. We noticed that the earth had also started to move. I couldn't stand up and neither could Allie Mary. She and I were holding each other up as we staggered back toward the house, giggling and chattering incoherently.

When Mom heard us, she ran outside to get us and immediately smelled the moonshine. When Uncle Crockett learned what we had done he was terrified, not knowing what Dad might do to him when he arrived home from work that night. Mom was nervously pacing the floor and wondering who was going to get killed because of that moonshine.

Granddad Stone went to the field with a bucket and milked a cow. He brought the hot milk to Mom, and she poured it in a cup and made both Allie Mary and me drink it. Finally, Allie Mary vomited and went to sleep. I was still awake, so Granddad walked me around and forced me to keep drinking hot cow's milk until I vomited. About the time that Dad was due to get off work, I fell asleep.

Uncle Crockett spent the next three years fearing that Dad would find out what happened. Then one day, somebody told Dad about it in a joking manner. I'm not sure he ever believed the incident actually happened.

Thankfully, after that experience I never wanted to drink or even smell alcohol again for the rest of my life.

———◇———

About three houses away from us lived Grover Hatfield, a rough and rowdy man who also had a large family. The Hatfield men drank moonshine, too. And sometimes when they were drunk, they would gather on the ridge of the mountain with their pistols and shotguns. Somebody would yell, "The Hatfields are up on the ridge with guns!" And the Dunfords, who were also drunk, would grab their guns and rush onto our property for a shootout with the Hatfields.

The Dunford clan and the Hatfield clan would curse and yell at each other, then fire shots back and forth. It was like the Wild West, with the Hatfields shooting from the ridge and the Dunfords shooting from behind our barn, our smokehouse, and even our home. They would shoot at each other until they ran out of ammunition; then they would break up and calmly go back to their respective homes.

The Hatfields and the Dunfords were all excellent marksmen, so they must have never intended to harm each other. If they had, they certainly would have killed each other. Granddad Dunford—nicknamed One-Eyed West because of the way he closed one eye and stood sideways to shoot—had a reputation for being the fastest and most accurate draw in the country.

Before he moved to West Virginia, Granddad was shot by four men who came to his home and accused him of reporting them to the local police for operating a moonshine still. The four men started shooting, and Granddad yelled for someone to throw him a gun. His daughter threw him the gun, and his first shot hit one of the men between the eyes and killed him. He wounded another man as they all galloped off on their horses. Granddad didn't serve time for the murder; in fact, the judge threatened to sentence him for not killing the other three. Granddad would sometimes pull up his shirt and let the grandchildren feel the two 38-caliber bullets that went through his body and were still lodged in his back from that shooting.

So when the Dunfords and the Hatfields had a shootout with each other, they must have either been shooting for sport, or too frightened of each other to actually do physical harm to one another. In one showdown, a Hatfield boy shot and superficially wounded a Dunford boy. He yelled, "They've shot me, they've shot me!" The Hatfields took off running.

The women could shoot, too.

Dad worked second shift in the mines, so he didn't leave work until 11:00 p.m. One night after dark, while Dad was still at work, someone came to our home and climbed up our chimney. Because of the triangular manner in which the stones were laid, it was possible to climb from the ground to the top of the chimney. From the top, someone threw a shirt into the chimney where it caught fire and smoked up our house. Aunt Ellen, Mom's sister, was visiting our home at the time. She yelled, "I'm gonna shoot somebody if you don't get out of here!"

The perpetrator came to the door and rattled the door knob, as though trying to get into the house. Aunt Ellen kept threatening to shoot but the doorknob kept rattling. So Aunt Ellen, making good on her threat, grabbed Dad's 12-gauge shotgun and stood a few feet from the door. She pulled the trigger and fired a shot that blasted a hole through the front door. Someone took off running, and Mom never had a problem like that again.

This was a rough place to live and raise a family.

CHAPTER 2

We Needed Revival

Over the next several years, Mom gave birth to four more children. Besides Lola, Morgan, Allie Mary, and me, we had three other sisters—Bertha, Rena, and Juanita—and a brother, William. Eventually our family grew by yet another brother, Lewis, and another sister, Brenda. Mom suffered a miscarriage with one child, and she gave birth to Bessie and Kenny, both of whom died at a young age.

We were now living in a larger home that Dad built for us on a plot of land that Granddad Stone gave us. The house, which was made from hewn, squared chestnut logs, was never large enough for the size family that we had. Situated in the valley and surrounded by mountains, it was a beautiful place to live. But we had to walk two miles to get from the house to the main road, so during a heavy winter snow, it was difficult for the children to get to school and for Dad to walk to and from his job in the mines. In a cold winter, sometimes it seemed that we would freeze to death before we arrived at our destination.

Dad's employer was Pond Creek Pocahontas Coal Company, and he worked at the Bartley Number One mine. On January 10, 1940, the children were outside playing in the yard while Mom sat on the porch with a woman who lived nearby. Suddenly they heard a deep rumble, almost like the sound of a continuous roll of thunder. Everyone stood motionless and listened quietly to the rumble that was coming not from the sky, but from deep inside the ground.

Mom's heart sank as she said, "Oh, dear God. The mine just blew up."

This was a shaft mine, and Dad was getting ready to go down the shaft just as it blew up. The wind pressure of the explosion propelled splinters of burned wood, paper, and other debris out of the mine shaft. Smoke and fire blew from the exit where the coal was brought up from the ground.

Dad did not come home from work that day. Three days passed and still we had neither seen nor heard from him. From the moment of the explosion, Mom paced back and forth, wringing her hands and crying. Finally, some of the neighbors asked our cousin Darrie to walk to the mine and find out what happened to his Uncle Bill.

When Darrie arrived at the mine, he learned that Dad was unharmed. But since he worked as an electrician and a mechanic, Dad had been stringing lights and helping with the rescue. He had worked virtually non-stop for three days, not thinking that perhaps Mom and the kids were wondering if he was even alive. When Dad found out how worried Mom was, a mine official sent him home. You can imagine how thrilled we all were to see him.

Ninety-one men died that day; only four miraculously survived. Almost every home in Bartley had flowers on the door, signifying that someone in the family had died. Many of Dad's friends were killed, and women and children were left without a husband or a father. The Bartley

Number One mine explosion was one of the greatest tragedies the area had ever experienced.

Around this time, Mom gave birth to a precious little baby girl who had a full head of black hair. She was named Bessie Virginia, after two of Mom's relatives. When Bessie was just a baby, one of Mom's relatives—a blind and very heavyset woman—was babysitting the children. She had Bessie cradled in her arms as she rocked her.

This woman had a chewing tobacco habit, and she spit her tobacco into a tin can that she kept on the floor. As she bent over to pick up the can, apparently the weight of her body injured Bessie internally, and we heard Bessie scream as though she had been badly hurt. She cried for a long time and, over the next two days, her body began to swell. Then she began to hemorrhage. Women who lived nearby came to our house, and I recall them using a cloth to wipe a gray substance that kept coming from Bessie's nose, ears, and mouth.

In those days the doctors made house calls. But since children were asked to leave when the doctor visited, I don't know if a doctor ever examined Bessie. But within a few days she died, and Dad built a small casket and buried her on the farm in the Stone family cemetery. The woman who was responsible for Bessie's death left our home and never returned.

Grandma Allie Dunford also became very sick and, although nobody knew what kind of illness she had, her body seemed to waste away. Shortly before she died, several of her daughters, including Mom, were in her home and at her bedside.

As the daughters gathered around her bed, Grandma Dunford tried with all the effort she could muster to raise herself off the bed as she said, "Children, move out of the way. That nice man at the end of the bed wants to come and talk to me. Would you please move from the foot of the bed?"

The girls looked around and didn't see anybody. But they obeyed and moved away from the foot of the bed. In just a short time, Grandma Dunford died. Uncle Rufus said that she was a believer in Christ when she died, and he was certain that the man she saw in the Spirit was an angel who had come to carry her soul and spirit away to heaven.

Grandma Dunford lived a difficult life on this earth. Raised as a Cherokee Indian, she then married Sam Dunford. She often said to him, "Shucks in a tobacco patch, Sam. You're gonna kill me with all that drinkin'. You're just gonna kill me."

———◇———

While all of this was happening to our family in the little town of Bartley, tragic events were occurring around the world. On December 7, 1941, Japanese fighters bombed our warships that were anchored at Pearl Harbor, and almost twenty-five hundred Americans were killed that day. Dad owned the only battery-operated Philco radio in Bartley, so men came to our home after work and listened for hours to the news reports. The children were not allowed to speak during those broadcasts. There was complete silence in the house while everybody in the room listened to reports of the destruction that was wrought by the attack.

During that time, Hitler and the German Nazis were forcefully invading Europe, killing millions of innocent people in the process.

On June 6, 1944, under the command of General Dwight Eisenhower, American and Allied troops entered France in the region of Normandy, and our country became embroiled in World War II.

During the war, the schools occasionally released the boys for an hour or more so that we could walk up and down the Dry Fork River and look for old tires and scraps of metal. The school collected the items that we found, and a government official picked them up so they could be recycled into weaponry.

I also recall that shoes were rationed. Even before rationing, Dad could afford to buy each of us only one pair of shoes at a time. But after the rationing, he made the boys go barefoot during the warmer months. I don't recall him making the girls go barefoot, but from at least May through October, the boys in our family did not wear shoes. If he caught us wearing shoes, he would say, "You get back in the house and take those shoes off. If you wear them out, what are you going to do this winter?" There were times in the late spring and early fall that we walked barefoot to school through patches of ice.

Though most rationing did not affect us, the government also rationed rubber, gasoline, and canned goods. New tire sales were prohibited. Even hamburger and butter had to be purchased with rationing stamps.

The war finally ended in 1945. The United States lost 407,000 soldiers during World War II; another 672,000 were wounded. My cousin Darrie Whittaker served in the army and was stationed in Germany. When he came home at the end of the war, he brought back a German woman that he claimed to have married while overseas.

The two of them lived with our family for a while, and I absolutely could not stand this woman. She was hateful and abusive to all the children, and my parents even made the girls give up their bed for Darrie and this woman. On one occasion, I mouthed off to her and she took both hands and slapped me on the sides of my head so hard that my head was spinning. It felt like she had burst my eardrums. I threatened to kill her if she ever touched me again.

After living with us for two months, Darrie took this woman someplace and she never returned. He wouldn't tell us where she went. He simply stated, "She's gone to meet some people she was supposed to meet."

Years later, I discussed this situation with people in our government, who thought that perhaps this woman was a Nazi who used Darrie to get into the United States as part of a group that escaped from Germany. No doubt she came here and stayed with Darrie as long as necessary before connecting with her fellow Nazis in America.

In those days, violence, alcoholism, tragic events, and a lifestyle of sin seemed to be accepted as a normal part of everyday life in the coal mining settlements. But God was getting ready to send an outpouring of the Holy Spirit to our community. Before long, revival would break through and spread like wildfire. The Lord knew how badly our lives needed transformation.

Morgan was the first person in our immediate family to accept Christ, but shortly before either he or I knew much of anything about salvation, we got into a fight that could have ended tragically.

Edgar Cline, a young man who was dating Lola and would later become my brother-in-law, was with Morgan in our home that day. I don't remember what triggered the fight, but Morgan belted me and I hit him in the stomach, knocking the air out of him. I ran through the house and grabbed Dad's leatherneck 22-rifle, jerked the clip out of it, and loaded it with about ten shells. I had a foul mouth and a temper, so I cursed as I went outside and dared Morgan to come near me.

Edgar said, "Morgan, you'd better get out of here. Freddie's mad and he's got a gun. He might kill you. I've never seen him that mad."

Morgan came outside and stood on the porch. He yelled, "I'll whip you and break your neck!"

"I'll shoot you if you lay a hand on me!" I threatened.

Morgan was about ten steps away from me, and he crouched to come toward me. I threw the gun up and pointed it right between his eyes. As I've already mentioned, we all knew how to aim and hit our target and, with my explosive temper, I was mad enough to kill him right there on the spot.

Before I could pull the trigger, I heard an audible voice in my right ear that said, "Fred, if you pull that trigger and shoot your brother, your life is ruined forever. Don't do that."

I raised the gun about a foot above his head and fired a shot. Edgar grabbed Morgan and jerked him away. Morgan was so shaken over the incident that he ran off and stayed gone for a week.

That shows you how the enemy works. Just before Morgan and I accepted Christ, the enemy tried to get us into a serious fight. If I had shot him, I surely would have killed him. I could have killed not just my brother, but the very person who was going to lead me to Jesus Christ. Morgan would have died lost, and I would have gone to prison and ruined my life. It was a supernatural act of God that He allowed either an angel or the Holy Spirit to speak audibly to me and warn me not to shoot my brother. Morgan is still alive today, and we are as close as two brothers can be. Thank God for His mercy and grace.

———◆———

I was about sixteen years old when the great coalfield revival broke out in southern West Virginia. A woman named Mildred Collins preached this revival that resulted in hundreds of people being saved and filled with the Holy Spirit.

Before Mildred accepted Christ, she often stood on the bank of the Dry Fork River and listened to the music and preaching as it drifted through the open windows of a little church on the other side of the riverbank. One time when the water level in the river was low, she and another woman crossed the river barefoot and attended a church service. Mildred returned the second night and gave her heart to Christ.

Mildred and others began to hold regular prayer meetings, asking the Lord to save the sinners in our area and to bring revival. Months later God called Mildred to preach, and she began a revival that was conducted at the Ballard Waldron Schoolhouse in Bartley Number One Valley. Even though it wasn't widely accepted for women to preach at that time, Mildred became such an anointed soul-winning evangelist that it didn't matter to anybody that she was a woman. In fact, over seventy men were called to preach under her ministry.

Later the services were moved to a small church near the railroad tracks in English, West Virginia to an area called Flat Top. Between the church at Flat Top and a church at Yukon, West Virginia, the revival lasted for three and a half years. There were services every single night; they stopped for nothing.

God poured out His Spirit mightily during that revival. Morgan and my cousin Darrie were the first people in our family to accept Christ during this revival, while it was still held at the schoolhouse.

Shortly after Morgan accepted Christ, he was lying on his bed in our sun porch, and he was shaking under the power of God. He was speaking in tongues, but I had no idea what it was. I cursed and said, "I need to get the corn hoed before Dad gets home from work, so get off the bed and quit that nonsense. Get outside and help me hoe this corn."

Morgan rose up from the bed, and ordinarily we would have gotten into a fight. But this time he said, "Fred, you can curse me if you want to. Say anything you want to about me. But don't say anything about the speaking in tongues that you heard me doing. That's the baptism of the Holy Ghost. This is a gift from God that I have. Don't say anything about that."

I didn't know anything about speaking in tongues or the baptism of the Holy Ghost, but I knew that Morgan had changed. His lifestyle and attitude had changed. He wasn't playing poker with me, he wasn't cursing, he wasn't drinking, and he wasn't getting into arguments and fights anymore.

Before long my sister Lola went to the revival and accepted Christ. Morgan pleaded with me to come to the revival, but I kept putting him off and making excuses.

Here is an example of what I would do. To earn money, Morgan and I looked for coal that was imbedded in slate and we cut the coal out, selling it in baskets along the side of the road. People gave us fifty cents for a basket of this coal, which was just enough to buy a ticket to see a movie at the local theater.

On the way to the church, you had to pass the theater. While Morgan headed to the revival, I stopped to see a movie. But Morgan was persistent and I was running out of excuses. He finally persuaded me to go to church with him one night. It was November of 1949.

I told Morgan that I was going to sit in the back of the church, and I told him to promise that he would not come back and talk to me. I had never been to church and had no idea that Morgan might come back and talk to me. But I'm certain the enemy was planting that in my mind to keep me from giving my life to the Lord.

I went to church with Morgan and sat in the back. A woman named Ruby Kingry sang and played the guitar as well as anybody I had ever heard, and she led the congregation in wonderful hymns of worship. Then Mildred Collins preached a sermon with a strong anointing. The convicting power of the Holy Spirit was in the service that night.

As Mildred gave the altar call, I heard her speak the following words: "Fred, if you should die at midnight tonight, where would you spend eternity? You are lost without God." She did not know me, and she later told me that she did not say that. Nobody else heard her say it, either.

Morgan came back to me with tears in his eyes. I had never seen Morgan cry, not even when Dad gave him a severe beating. I shook my head no, telling him that I wasn't interested. I looked away and headed toward the back door as Morgan turned and walked back toward the altar.

But once again, I heard those same words that seemed to come from Mildred's mouth as she spoke from the pulpit: "Fred, if you should die at midnight tonight, where would you spend eternity? You are lost without God."

About that time, Morgan turned around and came back to me and said, "Freddie, you're a sinner. You're a bad sinner. God loves you. I love you. And you need to be saved. Won't you come tonight?"

This time, the Holy Spirit spoke to my heart and I knew that I was a sinner bound for hell. I was gripped by the convicting power of the Holy Spirit; that night, I followed Morgan to the altar in that simple little coalfield church. The Christians at that altar showed me how to pray, and I gave my life to Christ. After praying for a few minutes at the altar, a great peace filled my heart and mind. I felt free at last! Thank God for a brother who led me to Christ and did not give up.

By the next day, word had gotten out that I had attended church and gone to the altar. One of the boys on the school bus said to me, "Hey, I heard you went to a Holy Roller church!"

I said, "Yeah, what of it?"

When we arrived at school and I got off the bus, I had walked about thirty steps when the boy who had been making fun of me on the bus threw a rotten apple. It hit me on my left shoulder and splattered on my books, my face, and my clothes. Before I went into the school, I laid my books down and waited on a wooden bridge that was about eight feet above the creek below.

A classmate whose mother attended a holiness church came by and said, "Fred, why did you put your books down? We need to get to class."

I said, "I'm waiting on the guy who threw the apple at me. I'm going to throw him headfirst into this creek."

"You can't do that," he told me. "You're a Christian now. You need to serve the Lord and live right. I don't know much about it, but my mother does. She lives right. Now go on to class and don't let that boy bother you. Let me take care of him."

Thank God for this young man. He was a sinner, but his mother must have lived a godly life around him. I picked up my books and went into the school. That was the last time I ever had a problem with any of the boys.

Almost every night, Morgan and I attended the Flat Top revival where the Lord was moving mightily. Mildred Collins always preached a simple message, but God gave her a powerful anointing to reach lost souls. Hardhearted grown men wept unashamedly as the power of God touched their lives. New converts praised God and gave personal testimonies with great boldness. Many of the teenagers at Big Creek High School were also being saved.

There was never a rush to leave the presence of God as people prayed for an hour or longer at the altar. There were always other believers there to encourage those who were seeking something from the Lord. It was a glorious revival.

Soon after my conversion, I began to seek God for the baptism of the Holy Spirit. Morgan had an experience that I didn't have, and I wanted whatever he had. I knew that it was possible to have more of God, and I wanted all that I could get.

I didn't know much about the baptism of the Holy Spirit, but I had heard some manifestations of it during the church services. For example, the Holy Spirit often operated through Elmer Jordan and his wife, two wonderful, godly people who fasted and prayed and were very close to the Lord. One would speak in tongues and one would interpret. This was the first time that I saw two spiritual gifts operating in the church. It was so inspiring that I looked forward to hearing this anointed couple speak a message in tongues and give an interpretation.

Many who had been saved during the revival were also receiving the baptism of the Holy Spirit. Though I desired this gift, I had no idea how to receive. Did I have to do something to receive the gift? What happens when a person receives this baptism? I knew nothing. So I simply went to the altar and prayed for whatever the other people had. I said, "Lord, whatever this is that everybody else has, I'd like to have it, too. It looks to me like I need it."

For the next three nights, I knelt at the altar in front of the pulpit and people gathered around to pray for me. On the third night of praying to receive this gift of the Holy Spirit, I felt a strong power come upon me—and it was a power that I could feel, not emotionalism or anything else. I felt it in my fingers, my hands, my arms, my chest, and finally all over my body.

Somebody told me to let go and let the Spirit take over. I had no idea what that meant. But soon I noticed that words of praise were coming out of my mouth, and they were in another language. I still wasn't sure what that was. Somebody who heard me speak told me that it was the baptism of the Holy Spirit.

After that, I felt more love and joy than I had ever felt in my life. I was overflowing with such love for everybody that I hugged every brother in the church. I ran all over the sanctuary praising God, and it seemed that I was floating in the air. As I ran, I kept bumping the wall of the church and thinking that I felt as though I might go right through the wall.

About two hours passed, but it seemed like five minutes. The pastor asked that someone who had been blessed of God testify. Before that night, I had been very shy and had not wanted to testify in church for fear of saying the wrong thing. But now I couldn't keep quiet. It felt like fire had touched my tongue, and I arose with a boldness I had never known. I wanted to tell everybody what God had done for me. If I could have told the whole world about this wonderful gift of salvation and the baptism of the Holy Spirit, I would have.

Several nights later, I was invited to attend the Yukon Church of God in Christ. Jack Griffith, a wonderful minister and Spirit-filled man of God, was the pastor of that church. They had a church bus that picked us up in Bartley. By the time the bus got back to Yukon, there was standing room only.

At that time I had no call to preach, but I was serving God, attending school, doing my chores at home, and attending church at night. In a service one night about 7:00, Pastor Griffith called everybody to come forward for prayer. An hour later, I was still at the altar praying. I felt compelled to continue praying, and I knew that I could not leave the altar. The pastor preached while I was still praying. Around 10:00, Pastor Griffith dismissed the service and said, "Would somebody like to stay with this young man while he prays?" Another young man named Al Collins, who later became a close friend of mine, sat next to me while I continued to pray.

Shortly after 11:00 p.m., I had a vision in which it seemed that I was carried away to the third heaven where I saw the top of the city of God. It shone with an incredible and indescribable brightness that seemed to light up the entire universe. I cannot find words in my vocabulary to describe what I saw. I can only say that it takes your breath away. As I viewed the city, the Holy Spirit within me was singing a song to glorify the city of God. Then the vision vanished.

When I stopped praying, Al Collins told me that I had started to sing in tongues. He asked me what happened while I was singing, and I told him about the vision. He said, "While you were singing, your face seemed to disappear behind the glow of a pure white light. Even your hair turned snow white. When you stopped singing, the glow vanished back into your skin."

The next night, Pastor Griffith said, "I want this young black-haired boy who prayed for so long last night to testify. God told me that He did something for him, and I believe there's a call of God on His life."

I was sitting on the front seat of the church, and I stood up to testify. The Spirit of God fell on me and when I came to myself, I was at the back door. I suppose I had been testifying for about five minutes, but I didn't even know what I said. All I know is that, after I finished speaking, I found myself all the way at the back door.

The pastor said, "Well, folks, I told you that God told me He did something for this young man. Does anybody doubt that he has been called to preach?"

About a week later, I was praying once again in this same church when I had another vision. In living color, I saw a beautiful, ornate door, but there was no door handle on the outside. The door could be opened only from the inside and, when it opened, there stood Jesus Christ. There was no doubt in my mind that it was Jesus.

He didn't say a word to me; He just opened the door and stretched both hands toward me. I reached out my hands toward Him, though

I never succeeded in touching His hands. Then, in a split second, He vanished.

I didn't tell anybody about that vision right away, but after that happened, Pastor Griffith began to call on me regularly to testify. Those two visions gave me an urge and an inspiration to preach. Pastor Griffith must have noticed that because he often asked me to speak. Thank God for a pastor who recognized the call of God on my life, and encouraged me and gave me that opportunity.

CHAPTER 3

Called to Preach

Revival spread throughout southern West Virginia, and many people were giving their lives to Christ and receiving the baptism of the Holy Spirit. The feuding clans of the Hatfields and the McCoys—and even a few of the Dunford men—were being convicted of their sins and giving their hearts and lives to the Lord. But many of the Dunford men were unconcerned about their spiritual condition and had no desire to accept Christ and allow Him to change their lives. Some were skeptics until the day they died.

In the area where I grew up, it was the mercy of God that brought revival and kept us all from killing each other. Before that revival, it seemed that somebody was getting beaten up, shot, or killed every week. Our lives desperately needed to be transformed by the power of the Holy Spirit.

Grover Hatfield—the neighbor who used to gather his relatives on the ridge above our house and have a shootout with the Dunfords—accepted Christ in Jolo, West Virginia at a church that his father attended. When I returned home from a revival service one night, I said, "Dad, in church tonight I heard that Grover Hatfield got saved."

Dad cursed and said, "I hope to God he did. That man has raised more hell in this holler than anybody I know of."

Not long after that, I was in a church service when Grover came forward to receive the baptism of the Holy Spirit. He was crying and shaking under the power of God. The minister laid hands on Grover and prayed, and the next thing I knew, Grover was speaking in tongues.

The next morning I told Dad that Grover Hatfield received the baptism of the Holy Spirit and spoke in tongues. This time Dad didn't curse. He said, "Fred, I thank God. I'm not living right myself, but I hope and pray Grover's changed. He sure needed it."

Dad would never see Grover Hatfield go back to his old lifestyle. For the rest of his life, Grover was a wonderful Christian man who served God mightily.

Shortly after Grover received the baptism of the Holy Spirit, Morgan and two of Grover's sons took the coon dog and went into the mountains above Grover's farm to hunt. About a half mile up the mountain, the dog spotted something. The guys were using flashlights, and all they could see were two eyes looking down at them from the top of a tall tree. Morgan was ready to shoot when one of the Hatfield boys said, "Let me shoot. I haven't had a chance to shoot tonight."

They told him to shoot, so he aimed and fired. Within seconds they heard a meow. Instead of a coon falling out of the tree, a cat fell out of the tree, right at their feet.

This was a beautiful Persian cat and one of the boys said, "Oh, no! That's Dad's cat! He'll beat us half to death for killing that cat!" The boys agreed to keep their mouths shut and not tell Grover or anybody else about the cat.

Two days later, a neighbor who was hunting saw the cat and brought it to the Hatfield home. He said, "Grover, I believe this is your cat. It sure looks like your cat."

Grover looked at it and said, "Yep, that's my cat."

He looked straight at the son who had fired the shot and calmly said, "That was a good old cat while she was living, wasn't she? Why don't you take that cat and give it a good burial?"

Morgan was in the Hatfield home to witness that exchange, and he rushed back home to tell us about it. He was panting as he ran inside and yelled, "Boy, I'll tell you one thing. Grover Hatfield's saved! If there ever was a Christian in this holler, it's Grover Hatfield!"

He told us the story of the cat, and we were all astonished, knowing the temper that Grover had before he was saved.

Throughout McDowell County, West Virginia, people like George Spears, Rufus Dunford, Lawrence Pruitt, Bill Addair, and Mildred Collins were preaching, and revival was still going strong. I was meeting and becoming friends with many young men who would later be called by the Lord to preach. One of them was Lloyd Addair, the son of Bill Addair. Lloyd and I are still good friends to this day.

I finally persuaded my sister Allie Mary to go to the revival with me one night. We were sitting together that evening and, after the sermon, I gave her an invitation to come to the altar and accept Christ. She went to the altar, and several of the women surrounded her to pray for her.

I was so excited that she went to the altar that I started shouting and praising God. I was in the aisle walking backwards and praising God with my arms lifted when I walked right out the door of the church. I stepped off the porch and fell backwards into a puddle with about three inches of water. I was lying in water and mud from the top of my head to the bottom of my feet. I lay there speaking in tongues and praising God and, after about ten minutes, I opened my eyes and saw the stars in the sky. Only then did I realize that I was outdoors.

I got up and walked back into the church where Al Collins met me just inside the door. He said, "Brother Freddie, you were lying in that mud puddle right there." He asked me to turn around, and there was not a drop of mud or water on me anywhere. Not even on my shoes. God even kept me from getting dirty or wet in that muddy water. He knew that I had to wear those clothes to school the next day, and He kept my clothes clean. To this day, I consider that a supernatural miracle.

The Lord was beginning to give me prophetic dreams and visions. In the year 1950, I was praying at the altar one night when I saw a vision of an army—a northern army and a southern army—that was coming together and clashing. I saw aircraft, machine gun fire, hand grenades, and other weapons. The northern army was beating down and defeating the southern army. About that time, I saw Americans joining the southern troops in this battle.

I mentioned the vision to Al Collins, and he told me that God had given me a vision of a war. It wasn't long before the Korean War broke out. Once the United States got involved in the war, my friends and I received draft notices and orders to come to the draft board in Beckley, West Virginia for an interview and a physical examination.

By this time, I had filed for my exhorters license with the Church of God so that I could become an evangelist. A minister and Church of God State Overseer by the name of G. W. Lane said to me, "Brother Stone, the Church of God needs preachers like you and Lloyd Addair. Do you want to go to war?"

I replied, "I'm willing to go. I'd like to be either a medic or a chaplain, or maybe do something in communications."

Reverend Lane said, "We'd like you to preach if you can. Go to the draft board and show them your credentials. If the army gets all of you guys, there'll be nobody left preaching for us."

I met with the draft board for an interview. They asked about my background, and then asked if I was willing to go if called. I told them that I was, and that I'd like to be a medic or a chaplain, if possible. They explained the process and told me about the school that I would have to attend before I would be considered for a medic or a chaplain position. They asked me to step outside the office while they had a discussion

The board talked for about twenty minutes before calling me back into the room. They told me, "The draft board has discussed this, and we have decided that you can do the country more good if you stay here to preach and pray for the troops. If we need you, we'll call you."

Even though I had a draft classification of 1-A, I never received a call to serve. The State Overseer considered it a miracle of God.

During this time, my good friend Al Collins had begun to have severe headaches that hurt so badly he could barely function. No matter how many aspirins he took to relieve the headaches, they would not subside.

One day while lifting timbers in the coal mines, Al collapsed. He woke up in the hospital, and that is when they discovered that he had brain cancer. His family didn't want to tell me that he had cancer; I only knew that he was sick. Within weeks he died, and someone came to tell me the news.

Al was one of the best friends I had in the church. I deeply regretted that I didn't know he was seriously ill and had not visited him before he died. Al felt a call to the ministry, and I could not understand why the Lord took him home before he could fulfill his call to preach. But after his death, I had an experience that I still consider the most unusual of my life.

In the mountains above our farm, Dad helped me build a small cabin that I furnished with a table and chair, a quilt and a pillow, and a lantern and a gallon of kerosene. This is where I went to study, pray, and spend time with the Lord. Except in the wintertime when it was too cold, I stayed there for two or three days at a time, praying and reading the Bible.

On one occasion, I was at the cabin, sitting outside in a cane back chair that I had leaned against the cabin wall. I was alone except for the birds and the Lord. I had been sitting in the chair reading my Bible for about thirty minutes when I heard footsteps in the leaves and turned to see who was there. Just as I turned around, I saw a hand reach right through the wall of the cabin and touch me on the head. Instantly, my Bible fell onto my lap, my head dropped, and I felt my spirit leave my body. I looked back and saw my body slumped in the chair against the cabin. I thought, "Oh, no. I just died! I must have had a heart attack or something. Nobody will come looking for me for two or three days."

I seemed to take off like a rocket. In a flash, I was out in the universe in the most beautiful and indescribable expanse of blue that I have ever laid my eyes on. I stopped and was standing on absolutely nothing; I was suspended in the space of the universe. There were no planets around; it was just a massive expanse of gorgeous, medium blue crystal sky for what seemed like millions of miles. The entire time, I could feel a presence with me, which I knew was the Holy Spirit.

As I stood in this expanse of blue, I saw a blinding ball of pure white light moving toward me. It started out small; then it grew larger and larger until it took on the form of a person. It moved toward me quickly; then suddenly the light vanished as it seemed to disappear into this person. There, a great distance from me, Al Collins appeared. I had no fear at all as I thought to myself, "Oh my goodness! There's Al Collins!" I sensed that he was on a mission.

The Holy Spirit spoke to me and said, "God has sent Al Collins to give you a message."

At that moment, Al raised his right hand and said to me, "Brother Freddie, God has sent me to tell you that you must preach."

I tried every way to speak to him, but of course I could not. He repeated the message: "Brother Freddie, God has sent me to tell you that you must preach." Then he turned around and moved into a pure white light. He moved so quickly that, in the blink of an eye, he vanished.

The Spirit of God turned me around and, very quickly, I traveled feet first back to earth. Then my spirit entered my slumped over body. My entire body was shaking and the hair on my head was standing straight up. I wasn't shaking from fear; it was simply my body reacting to the presence of God. I sat in the chair for at least two hours before I got up because it seemed like I was stuck to that spot. I couldn't move until something supernatural lifted off me. I could only sit there and think about what had just happened.

After that incident, I knew without a doubt that the Lord wanted me to preach. I had been reading the Bible, praying, and fasting. But after that experience, I spoke about the Lord every time I had an opportunity. And sometimes the opportunity came through my good friend Billy Hale.

Billy would sometimes put a speaker on his car and drive around playing Christian music on 78-rpm records. He played country gospel artists like Bill Monroe and Mollie O'Day to attract attention; then he would introduce me by saying, "I've got Brother Freddie Stone here, and he's going to read some scripture and testify." We did that several times, driving up and down hollows and coalfields.

The fire of God was moving into Kentucky, and ministers from our area traveled into that state to conduct revivals. Mildred Collins and Ruby Kingry traveled to Shelbiana, Kentucky where they set up a tent and started a revival. Mildred preached, and Ruby sang and played the guitar. A young man named Chester Hurst attended the revival with the intent to mock and disturb the service. But the Holy Sprit convicted him and he went to the altar that night. He gave his heart to Christ, was filled with the Holy Spirit, and was soon called by the Lord to preach.

I met Chester when he came to Flat Top, West Virginia to preach. He and I would soon become friends and remain so until his death in 2005.

Chester lived in Kentucky at that time, and he sent me a money order for seven dollars so that I could travel by bus to Drift, Kentucky and help him in a revival. I had never traveled anywhere in my life, and I had no way to carry my clothes except in a paper bag. So Dad took me to an Army Navy store in War, West Virginia and bought me a metal suitcase. I took the seven dollars, caught a bus, and traveled for the first time in my life. When I arrived in Kentucky, Chester met me at the bus station and we started a revival.

Chester did most of the preaching, but I preached two nights. After the revival, Chester and the pastor of the church baptized over twenty new converts in a creek. It was Chester who gave me my first opportunity to preach in a revival.

———————◇———————

The United States was still fighting in the Korean War, and many of my buddies were serving overseas. In fact, almost every person I knew who was my age had been drafted and gone to war. In later years, I asked people who worked at draft boards why so many of the sons of coal miners were drafted. I was told, "The army knew that every coal miner's son could shoot a gun, hunt, and fight. Most of you were raised rough, and all of you could get the rank of sharp shooter almost immediately. That's what they were looking for—fighters."

Over fifty-four thousand men were killed during the Korean War, and over eight thousand were missing in action. Some were transported into camps in the Soviet Union and left there to die. Dale Smith and C. N. Morgan, both buddies of mine, were missing in action. Their families didn't know if they had been taken prisoner, or if they had been killed and their bodies never recovered. I was burdened for them, so I started to pray.

One night I had a dream in which I was standing about ten feet above ground, and I could see over the heads of people. There were old huts all around, and everything was muddy, dirty, and wet. I saw men who were standing in mud halfway up their boots as they looked out from behind barbed wire fences. I saw an American soldier standing with his hands on the barbed wire, and he seemed to be in deep thought. It was Dale Smith.

In this dream he said to me, "Freddie, my mother is worried about me. I want you to go tell her that I am in a North Korean prisoner of war camp. If she will pray for me, I will live to get out of this place." Immediately the prison camp vanished and I awoke.

I wrote this dream in a diary and went to the Church of God in Atwell, West Virginia to see Dale's mother. I said, "Sister Smith, I'm a friend of Dale's. He and I went to school together at Bartley Junior High and Big Creek High School. You're wondering about Dale, and I want to tell you a dream that I had. If this dream is of God, your son is not dead. He is in a prisoner of war camp, and he'll live to get out if you'll pray for him."

I told her the dream. She broke down and started crying, then immediately went to the altar to pray.

Several weeks later, I was preaching in another part of West Virginia. It was during the time that Dwight Eisenhower was running against President Truman, and the war was really bogged down. I came home from this revival and the bus pulled up at the station in Welch. I got off the bus and decided to pick up a newspaper. The headlines of the Welch Daily News read, "Two Local Men Released in Pan Mon Jon Prisoner Exchange."

I put a coin in the machine and got the paper. There on the front page were the high school pictures of Dale Smith and C. N. Morgan. Not a day passed that I had not prayed for those boys.

Earlier in the book I mentioned Darrie Whittaker, my cousin who brought the German woman to America after World War II, and then accepted Christ about the same time Morgan did. Uri Davidson, the man who came to Dad's rescue during the fight in the creek years earlier, was Darrie's stepfather.

Darrie had been a strong Christian at one time, but later he turned his back on God and was living in a backslidden condition. He had a root of bitterness and anger that ate away at his soul. Darrie had become critical of the church, but he went with me this particular night. During our conversation, without realizing that I had quoted scripture from Acts 8:23, I said, "Darrie, I perceive that you are in the gall of bitterness and the bond of iniquity."

During the altar service that night, Mildred Collins came to Darrie and urged him to come back to Christ and let the Lord restore him. He refused. Three days later, Darrie shot his stepfather Uri in the head at point blank range and killed him.

Darrie went to Granddad Dunford's house and confessed to what he had done. Granddad sent him to our house. Dad wasn't home from work at the time, so Darrie came to the house but didn't tell anybody what happened. He simply walked the floor as though he was troubled. Mom, who was about a week away from giving birth to my sister Brenda, asked him what was wrong but he wouldn't say.

Finally Dad came home from work where he had already heard about the shooting. Uri Davidson was one of the best friends Dad ever had, and when he saw Darrie on the porch, he went into a rage, cursing and threatening him.

I was digging potatoes in the field, and my future brother-in-law, Edgar Cline, rushed to get me. He said, "Darrie killed Uri and he's at the house right now. Bill is really having a fit. I'm afraid he might shoot Darrie. Get down there as quick as you can."

Immediately I rushed to the house. As soon as I got there, I asked Darrie if I could pray with him. He replied, "It's too late for that now. I should have prayed when you asked me in church the other night."

That taught me something about backsliding. You never know what might happen to somebody when they turn their back and walk away from the Lord. Jesus told us to stop sinning or something worse might happen to us. He also told us in Luke 11:24-26 what happens when an unclean spirit leaves a man. The spirit goes through dry places seeking rest. When it finds none, it takes seven other spirits more wicked than himself, and they will try to enter and dwell in the same man. If they succeed, the man will be much worse off than he was the first time.

I believe it was strongholds of bitterness, anger, and resentment, that caused Darried to turn his back on the Lord. Just three days after being urged to give his life back to Christ, he found himself sitting in the McDowell County jail facing a murder charge.

We all loved Darrie, and it was such a tragedy that he allowed bitterness, conflict, and anger to wreck his life. I talked to him after he was released from prison, but nothing that he said—even years later—ever gave me the impression that he repented and turned back to the Lord.

The enemy wants people to believe that God will never forgive them for all of the sins they have committed. But God would have forgiven Darrie for killing his stepfather if Darrie had only repented and asked forgiveness. When Jesus was crucified, He went to the cross in the place of a killer named Barrabbas. I'd like to think that even Barrabbas eventually realized that Jesus gave His life on the cross for him, dying in his place so that he could be free.

Darrie died years ago, and what a sad situation if he died without turning his life back to the Lord. I hope and pray that he did, but only God knows.

My brother Morgan also had an encounter that caused him to turn from Christ. During a church service one night, the assistant pastor's son came to the church with a loaded pistol. During the altar service, he waved the gun, cursed, and shouted, "These Holy Rollers talk about going to heaven! I'll see if I can't send a few of them to heaven tonight!"

Morgan knew that this guy had probably been drinking, so he grabbed the gun, shoved it in the guy's stomach, and yelled for help. Since I was praying at the altar, I was oblivious to what was happening. The pastor saw it and called for some of the men who were praying to help Morgan. But instead of making the young man leave the church and go home, the pastor let him continue to stand in the church and curse.

Then the guy punched Morgan in the face so hard that it nearly knocked some of his teeth out. Morgan took his jacket off and threw it on a seat, then told the boy to go outside with him. The pastor didn't rebuke the boy, perhaps because he was the assistant pastor's son. Instead, he told Morgan to go home. Then he asked somebody to take the other boy home.

The following night, this boy came back to church with a hunting knife. Once again, he cursed, took God's name in vain, and threatened people with the knife. Word got out that you'd better not go to that church because they bring guns and knives and you might get killed. I knew that kind of reputation would destroy the church, because nobody is going to attend a church where the pastor allows somebody to bring guns and knives to church and threaten people. Sure enough, it nearly destroyed the church.

Morgan learned that the incident was over petty jealousy. The boy was interested in a girl who attended the church, and he thought the girl had a crush on Morgan. So Morgan decided it would be best if he stopped attending that church. Gradually he dropped out of church altogether; and from there, he drifted far away from the Lord. Morgan carried anger and bitterness toward this boy for decades.

One thing that always bothered me about Morgan's situation was that nobody from the church, not even the pastor, ever visited Morgan to encourage him to get back in church. In the parable of the lost sheep, Jesus taught that if a man has a hundred sheep and one goes astray, he should leave the ninety-nine and go seek the one that is straying. I never saw the pastors, who are supposed to be the shepherds of the flock, go after any of the sheep that strayed.

———◇———

In faith, I was still stepping out to speak and evangelize. My friend Lloyd Addair and I became ministry partners and we traveled to preach revivals together. He and I had some interesting experiences in our early years of ministry.

When we were not evangelizing, we tried to have prayer meetings in the homes of people we knew. Lloyd and I both knew the Brickey family, and we told Mrs. Brickey that we would come to her home for a prayer meeting if she would invite some people over.

She invited several people and, shortly after everybody arrived, Mr. Brickey came home drunk. He walked in and, slurring his words, he cursed and said, "What's going on in here? What are these people doing in this house?"

I prayed silently, "God, give me wisdom."

The Spirit of the Lord said to me, "Give him a chair."

While I was getting a chair, I said to him, "Mr. Brickey, you know Bill Stone, up on the hill? He's my dad."

"Bill Stone? Is that your daddy?"

"Yes, he is. Here, have a seat. I'm getting ready to testify and read some scriptures."

He swore and said, "Oh well, go ahead."

I spoke, and Lloyd and I laid hands on a few people and prayed. Mr. Brickey started to cry. At first, I thought they were simply a drunkard's tears. But I said, "Mr. Brickey, you need the hand of God in your life. Why don't you give your life to Christ? You have a good wife and two little kids."

He agreed. Lloyd and I laid hands on him and started praying for the Lord to break the alcoholic spirit. Within two minutes of praying for him, he was as sober as he could be. The smell of whiskey that almost knocked you down when he walked in the door completely disappeared.

The Lord miraculously took every bit of that alcohol out of his body. He accepted Christ that night and started going to church with his family.

That incident proved to me that, even though a person can be high on drugs or drunk on alcohol, God can break the spirit and take every bit of that from their body instantly. He can set them free that quickly.

* * *

Things didn't always go so well for us. I recall the time that Lloyd and I traveled to Allen, Kentucky and borrowed an old, worn and rotted tent from an evangelist. We spent a whole day putting up the tent and planned to start services the following night. But the next day, a great wind and rain storm hit, knocking the tent over and completely destroying it. The evangelist who owned the tent charged us a hundred dollars because the tent was destroyed.

Lloyd and I didn't have any money, and we weren't going to be making any money in this revival because now we had no place to preach. Granddad Dunford loaned me fifty dollars, my share of the cost, and I repaid him ten dollars a month. That was the last time we rented a tent. We decided to rent buildings from then on.

In the summer of 1952, we rented a community building and started a revival in Panther, West Virginia. In the Appalachian Mountains, there was a church group that handled rattlesnakes and copperheads during their services. Snake-handling was a strange doctrine that had a stronghold on this group of people; some lost hands, arms, and even their lives from handling these snakes.

I was aware of an incident involving a snake-handler that occurred during a revival that Mildred Collins preached in Kentucky. While people were praying during the altar service, a man placed a box that contained a snake at the bottom of the platform stairs. Mildred would have been forced to step over the box to leave the platform. Since the entire church was praying, nobody noticed what this man had done. But during the altar service, the Holy Spirit gave a message in tongues with this interpretation: "You have brought into this church that which I have cursed. If you do not remove it immediately, I will bring swift judgment upon you." This message was given twice. Mildred had no idea what that message was about until this man came forward, picked up his snake in a box, and quietly left the building with his head hung in shame.

Lloyd and I didn't know that this community building we were renting for a revival was also the building that a snake-handling church used for their services.

The revival wasn't going as well as we hoped, so we sought the Lord to learn the reason. One night, the Lord gave me a dream. In this dream, a man walked up and handed me a coconut that looked good on the outside. Then he handed me a hammer. When I took the hammer and broke open the coconut, I saw that it was rotten inside. God was revealing to us that the revival was going to be spiritually worthless at that time.

Sure enough, the revival was fought in every way imaginable. The pastor of the snake-handling church that normally met in this building wanted to have the building back for a church service. We closed the revival rather than be in the building after a snake-handling preacher had held a service.

Months later, Lloyd and I went back to this same location and tried again. This time, God gave us a good revival and the building filled up each night. We learned that the snake-handling people were getting worried about the success of the revival. One night, two men drove up, and one of the men got out of the car and came inside. He said to Lloyd and me, "Brother Roberts wants to know if he can come to your revival."

He seemed to think that we knew who Brother Roberts was, but we did not. So we said, "Sure, everybody's welcome to come to this revival."

He went outside and spoke with the driver of the car. Then he came back inside and said to us, "Brother Roberts wants to know if he can bring his serpents inside."

"Serpents?" we asked.

"Yes. Brother Roberts has two serpents in the trunk of his car, and he wants to know if he can bring them in and handle the serpents during the service."

Lloyd looked at me and I looked at him. We were two young preachers who had no experience dealing with anything like that. I quickly prayed for wisdom to know how to respond to this man.

The Holy Spirit said to me, "Tell this man exactly what I tell you to say."

I turned to my left, and sitting on the third seat was a woman who had a huge goiter on the front of her neck. I opened my mouth to speak and, not knowing what would come out, said to this man, "Do you see that woman with the goiter on her neck? We're going to pray for that woman tonight. Tell Roberts that there's a woman in here with a goiter as big as a baseball. Tell him that if he can pray a prayer of faith for that woman's healing, then tomorrow night he can bring his serpents."

He left, went to the car, and returned with a message: "Brother Roberts said that where the power of God isn't welcome, he isn't welcome."

By that time I had boldness. I said, "You tell Roberts that God Almighty is going to judge him for calling two snakes in the trunk of his car the power of God."

I thought maybe the two of them would come back inside and mop the floor with Lloyd and me, but they left and never returned.

CHAPTER 4

Miracles in My Early Ministry

During the decades of the 1940s and early 1950s, great revivals were breaking out all across America. Men like Oral Roberts, Thea Jones, T. L. Osborne, and others were preaching and seeing miracles throughout the United States and other parts of the world. God poured out His Spirit and extraordinary healings were taking place. We saw this in our own revivals as well.

Lloyd and I began a revival in Shelbiana, Kentucky at a small church on the railroad yards. We vowed that we would visit every house in town and invite people to the revival.

We were walking door to door when we came upon a little black tarpaper shack. We knocked on the door. When the woman answered, I noticed a terrible odor which I immediately thought was the smell of rotten flesh. We learned that the woman's sister was in this tiny one-room house, lying on a cot beside a potbellied stove, and she was dying. We told her that we believed in praying for the sick and asked if we could come inside and pray for her.

She invited us inside to pray for her sister, whose right side of her face had been eaten away by cancer. Part of her nose and ear were gone, and the cancer was moving to her eye. The flesh of her cheeks was decayed to the bone. Even the roots of her teeth were visible.

We witnessed to the woman, read scriptures about divine healing, and anointed her with oil. We prayed over her and cursed the cancer, praying that the cancer cells be destroyed. The ladies thanked us for praying and we left.

Two days later, we were conducting the church service and I was just getting ready to introduce Lloyd before he came to preach. A woman in the congregation stood up and said, "Brother Stone, everybody in this church knows about the woman with cancer who lives up in the holler. She was supposed to be dead in a week or two, and I heard she had been healed. I just went by to see her before church, and she said that two doctors—a young heavyset doctor and a tall, skinny black-haired doctor—came by and opened up a bottle, put something on her face, and prayed for her. She was healed. I saw for myself that there is no cancer on her face. The woman's face looks like a newborn baby's skin."

Neither Lloyd nor I said a word about praying for the woman two days earlier. We weren't smart enough to know that if we had given God the glory for that healing, we might have had the greatest revival that area had ever seen. We were so afraid that somebody would try to give us the credit, and we knew that it was God who brought the healing. But instead of keeping quiet about it, we should have told the church about the prayer and given God the glory.

God also moved miraculously during a great revival in Martin, Kentucky. Before I went to that town for a revival, I had a dream in which a man walked up to me and said, "Son, what are you looking for?"

I replied, "I'm looking for a place to preach."

In this dream the man said, "The saints in Martin, Kentucky need you. If I tell them you're coming, will you go there to preach?"

After that dream, I wrote a letter to a minister I had preached for in Kentucky named Reverend Bart. I told him I'd like to come to Martin, Kentucky for a revival. I didn't even know if there was a town by that name, but he wrote back and said, "I called someone that I know in Martin, and Osborne's Chapel wants you to come for a revival."

I traveled to Martin and held a revival at Osborne's Chapel. During this revival, I prayed, fasted, studied the Bible, and read a book by T. L. Osborne entitled, *Healing the Sick and Casting Out Devils*. Ray Fraley, a friend from the Pentecostal Assembly in Drift, Kentucky came to visit, and he and I prayed until 5:00 one morning for this revival. At one point during that prayer, I was under such an intercessory burden for this revival that I felt like my chest would burst open. I had no idea at the time that it was an intercessory burden, and I even asked Ray to pray for me because I thought there was something physically wrong with me.

During the service that following night, I preached on divine healing. Between the study, prayer, fasting, and T. L. Osborne's book, I went into this revival with such a boldness to pray for miracles that I almost felt like telling people to bring the dead to church for prayer. After I preached the sermon on divine healing, I offered to pray for the sick. A gentleman who had been born blind in his left eye came forward for prayer. I saw nothing but white tissue in his eye socket. He was also crippled in one leg from a bone disease and he walked with a cane.

I prayed one time for his eye and nothing happened. Two Pentecostal preachers stood in the back of the church with their arms folded and watched me pray, but neither prayed nor offered to pray with me. There was so much unbelief in the congregation that I had to pray twice.

During the second prayer, I felt an anointing like a spark of electricity shoot through my arm and hand as I touched this man's eye and prayed for him. I covered his good eye and asked him to look at the ceiling toward the light. At first he could see nothing. Then I watched as the tissue covering his eye broke as though it had been cut by a knife. Then the tissue rolled across his eye like a scroll. After it rolled all the way across his eye, it vanished, leaving him with a perfect eye.

The man started yelling, "I can see! I can see!" Before long, everybody in the church was praising God except the two Pentecostal preachers who had been standing in the back with their arms folded. After the Lord healed the man's eye, I laid hands on his leg and prayed. He threw the cane over his shoulder and danced on that leg all over the church, praising God with a loud voice. Those two miracles were the catalyst for a great move of God during that revival.

God was giving both Lloyd and me a supernatural ministry but we didn't understand what to do with it. When Lloyd and I returned home to West Virginia after a revival, we told our pastor about the miracles we had seen. Instead of encouraging us to stay close to the Lord and let Him use us in ministry, he said, "Don't get the big head, boys. Better watch. When God starts using you like that, you might get proud and egotistical and lose out with the Lord."

His comments threw cold water all over me. I had to go back to my cabin in the woods and fast and pray to get my faith level restored. I know it's possible to get proud, but what was I going to be proud of except the grace of God and the power of the Holy Spirit?

Thankfully, I had good mentors who never knew they were mentoring me. I read everything by T. L. Osborne that I could get my hands on. And Thea Jones was one of the most outstanding Bible teachers and miracle workers of his day. When Thea came to Yukon for a tent revival, he shook the coalfields for God. Two thousand people filled the tent each night, and when he prayed for people, God performed instant miracles. Thea touched goiters, rebuked them, and commanded them to leave. Instantly the goiters would vanish. He prayed for people who had tumors that were visible through their clothing, and the power of God struck those people and their tumors disappeared instantly.

One of Thea's great miracles was when he prayed for a boy whose eye socket was white because he had been born without an iris and a pupil. Thea prayed, and witnesses on the platform watched as the invisible hand of God drew a pupil and an iris on the solid white portion of the boy's eye! The boy was healed that night by the power of Almighty God!

Thea said that the key to miracles and a great move of God was fasting and prayer. Before he began his ministry, he fasted for twenty-one days.

Another very good mentor was my Uncle Rufus Dunford. He prayed every morning, and it was never a quick prayer. He would generally begin by praying the Lord's Prayer; then he would pray in the Spirit. He never prayed only in English. I always enjoyed traveling to revivals with Rufus because he preached under an anointing that was so powerful, you would have to see it to believe it. When he started shaking and dancing under the power of God, the Holy Spirit would move across the entire congregation.

Rufus could pray a powerful prayer for sinners to receive salvation. He prayed with my Granddad Matt Stone after he was almost killed in an accident. Granddad was cutting down a tree when the tree dislodged and slammed him against another tree, causing severe internal injuries. We knew it was only a matter of time before he died. Granddad Stone was thought to be close to a hundred years old at that time, and he had never accepted Christ. But after Rufus talked to him and prayed for him, Granddad accepted Christ and was baptized before he died.

Rufus could also lay hands on people and they would receive the baptism of the Holy Spirit. The power of the Holy Spirit seemed to flow right out of his hands and into the people he prayed for. It was common for people to receive the baptism of the Holy Sprit when he laid hands on them and prayed. He also saw the Lord perform many miracles of healing during his ministry. I saw one of those great miracles when I accompanied Rufus to a revival at a small Pentecostal church in Beefhide, Kentucky where Teddy Wright served as pastor.

During that revival, a young boy about ten years of age came forward for prayer. He had been born with a club foot, so he was walking on his anklebone. Rufus prayed and nothing happened. He announced that he and I were going to fast and pray the next day, and he asked the parents to bring the boy back the following night.

Rufus and I fasted the next day and prayed for several hours. The parents returned that night with the little boy, and Rufus prayed for him. He prayed in the Spirit as he held this little boy's foot. After about two minutes of prayer, the boy's foot started turning until it became completely straight! Never in his lifetime had this boy walked on the bottom of his foot. But after Rufus prayed, God healed the boy's foot and it became perfect. The little boy ran to the door and back several times, walking for the first time on the bottom of a foot that was now normal. Rufus asked the boy to tell everybody what the Lord had done for him, but the boy was so happy that he didn't know whether to laugh or cry.

I loved to see these great healing miracles, and I believe that is one reason the Lord gave me the desire to pray for the sick. You can't experience miracles like that without wanting to pray for the sick and see God perform great acts of healing. Even sinners want to see miracles. During these great healing revivals, the ministers would stop in the middle of a healing service and ask for those people who wanted to accept Christ to come forward for prayer. Sinners packed out the altars.

Around 1953, I accompanied Rufus to a revival at the Christian Church of God in Esserville, Virginia where Gordon Freeman served as pastor. As the congregation sang, an elderly woman sitting on the front row took off her shoes and tucked them under the seat. Rufus looked at me and said, "This is going to be a tremendous service tonight."

"How do you know?" I asked.

He replied, "See that lady on the front row? That's Grandma Fields. She's a very devout child of God. Did you see her take her shoes off and tuck them under the seat? When the Spirit of the Lord is ready to be poured out, that is the first thing she does. The next thing she'll do is take the pins out of her hair and let it down. Then she'll stand up and start walking and praising the Lord. Every time that happens, the Lord pours the Holy Ghost out in the service."

Sure enough, after she took off her shoes, she took the pins out of her hair. Then she stood up. She started dancing before the Lord and walking the aisles around the church. When she got halfway around the church, she turned and started back to her seat.

Rufus said to me, "Do you see that golden oil that's flowing out from under her feet?"

I replied, "No, I don't see anything." The Lord had shown Rufus something in the Spirit realm that I could not see.

He said, "When this oil flows, the Holy Ghost is being poured out. Watch what happens when it starts hitting peoples' feet."

I didn't see the oil, but the Lord showed me a white cloud that started flowing across the floor, almost like vapor from dry ice. As it touched peoples' feet, they began to stand to their feet and rejoice and praise the Lord. In a moment's time, nearly every person in the church was on their feet praising the Lord. That was a fascinating thing to watch in the Spirit realm. An elderly woman who obeyed the Holy Spirit brought a tremendous blessing to the congregation that night. It was such an outstanding service that nearly fifty years later, people who had been in the service still talked about it.

Divers (or different) kinds of tongues is a gift of the Holy Spirit. It was divers tongues that allowed Rufus to minister to immigrants in their own language, even though he, in the natural, was unable to speak any of those languages.

I saw firsthand the gift of divers tongues through Rufus when he and I traveled to this same revival in Esserville. As we were driving into the city of Norton, Rufus stopped the car in front of a shoe repair shop. He got out of the car and put a coin in the parking meter.

"Why are we stopping here?" I asked.

"The Lord told me that I need to witness to a German in this shop. He is going to be taken from this life shortly, and God wants to give this man one more chance to get his life right with Him."

I said, "Do you know this man?"

He surprised me when he said, "No, I've never seen him. The Spirit of God just told me to go in there and witness to him."

Rufus walked into the shoe repair shop and I followed behind him. Rufus always wore a hat. He tipped his hat and, speaking in the German language, said to the man, "Good morning, sir. How are you doing this fine morning?"

The Holy Spirit gave me the interpretation of everything that was being said by both men as they spoke, even though I did not know the German language. I understood as the man answered, "I'm doing alright. How are you?"

This led to a conversation, and Rufus started witnessing to the man and telling him the entire plan of salvation. He talked about the birth of Christ and how He ministered and was crucified. He talked about how that Christ rose from the dead and ascended back to the Father. Then he asked the man if he was serving the Lord.

The man stared at Rufus for a few seconds before asking, "Are you a Catholic priest?"

In German, Rufus replied, "No."

"Are you a Jewish rabbi?"

"No."

In anger, the German cursed God and said, "If you're not a priest, and you're not a rabbi, then you must be one of those Holy Rollers."

When the man picked up a hammer and pointed it toward us, Rufus said, "Good day, sir. I have obeyed the Lord." Then he turned to me and said, "Come on, son. Let's go. I'll explain what happened when we get outside."

We both walked out and I asked, "If the Lord sent you to witness to that man, why did we leave so soon?"

Rufus answered, "Fred, the Lord wanted to send him a message of salvation before it's too late. He rejected it. That man had a spirit of rage that was going to turn on us. If we hadn't left when we did, he would have physically assaulted us. The Lord said that this man is a spiritual swine."

My first personal experience with the gift of divers tongues happened while I was walking down the street in Welch, West Virginia. A young man named Truman Smith, the son of a Church of God pastor, introduced me to a young man whom we called Tony the Greek. His parents owned a Greek restaurant in the town of Welch.

Tony, Truman, and I were walking down the street, and I was trying my best to talk to Tony. But since he didn't speak English very well, he and I had a language barrier. I knew about the gift of divers tongues, so I prayed and asked the Lord to let me speak something clearly to Tony.

The Spirit of the Lord said to me, "Do you have the same gift of the Holy Ghost that I gave to the church on the day of Pentecost?"

I replied in my mind, "Yes, Lord, I'm bound to have the same Spirit as the day of Pentecost."

"What did they do on the day of Pentecost?"

"They spoke many languages."

"If they spoke many languages, do you think I can give you the power to speak to Tony in his language?"

Faith rose up and, in my mind, I said, "Yes, Lord, I believe that you can give me the power to speak to Tony in his language."

I took a small Bible out of my shirt pocket, and it fell open to the twenty-third Psalm. I stopped Tony and Truman on the street and told Tony that I wanted to say something to him. When I opened my mouth, I was speaking Greek. As I continued to read, I went from speaking Greek, to speaking German, to speaking Italian. I had no idea at that moment what languages I was speaking.

After I read through the twenty-third Psalm, Tony took both Truman and me by the arm. He said to Truman in broken English, "You lie. You lie to me."

Truman replied, "Tony, I'm your friend. I wouldn't lie to you."

With his heavy accent, Tony said, "You tell me this boy no go to school to preach. He go to school! You say he no go to school to learn to preach!"

Truman said to me, "Freddie, have you been to school to learn to preach?"

I said, "No, Truman, I haven't been to school to learn to preach."

Tony said, "That cannot be. You speak to me in Greek. I speak German and Italian, and you speak to me in both languages. You don't wait; you speak in other languages like that." He snapped his fingers to indicate that I spoke with a smooth transition from one language to another. "I have to stop and think before I can speak in another language. But you don't wait. How do you do that?"

I opened the Bible to Acts chapter two and read about the people who were gathered together on the Day of Pentecost when the sound of a mighty rushing wind came from heaven and filled up the house. Tongues, as of fire, sat upon each one and they began to speak with other tongues as the Spirit gave them utterance. I explained to Tony that this was a supernatural gift of God that comes upon people.

That was the last time I ever saw Tony. Not long after that, his parents sold the restaurant and moved away.

Thirty years later, I was preaching at a church in Pearisburg, Virginia where I told this story. When I finished, I heard a voice with a heavy Greek accent coming from the back of the church. "Oh, that's my Tony! That's my Tony!" the woman exclaimed.

A petite, dark-haired woman stood up and I asked her to come forward. I said, "Sister, are you talking about Tony the Greek from Welch, West Virginia?"

She replied, "Yes, that's my Tony."

Incredibly, this was Tony's sister. She told us, "I never met you, but Tony said he met this skinny black-haired preacher. It was you. He came home and said, 'There was a preacher that talked to me today about Jesus Christ. He spoke to me in Greek, German, and Italian. He never spoke those languages before. He said the Spirit of God gave him the words.'"

I asked, "Is Tony still alive?"

"No, he died of a heart attack two years ago."

"Did he give his heart to Christ before he died?" I asked.

"Oh yes, he lived for God for many years."

"Did he have the gift of the Holy Spirit?"

"Yes, he had the gift!"

What a miracle that, thirty years later, I met Tony's sister in a church after telling this story! It was such a blessing to hear her testimony.

———◆———

While I was away from home conducting revivals, Mom gave birth to a baby boy, Kenny Edgar, who was named after two of my brothers-in-law. When he was born, there didn't appear to be anything wrong with him. But when he was about six months old, he would often tremble and scream as he clutched his chest.

Doctors at Grace Hospital X-rayed him and checked everything they could possibly check. They found nothing wrong with him, so they could not explain why he suffered like this every day.

By this time, Mom and Dad had moved into a larger, two bedroom house. When I came home from revivals, I usually slept on a cot in the corner of the second bedroom. During one visit home, Kenny had been crying from the pain for quite a while, so I asked Mom if I could hold him and care for him while she and Dad tried to get some sleep.

Mom said, "Well, he does stop crying when you hold him. I don't understand that. As long as you are holding him, he won't cry. And if he is crying, he stops when you pick him up. He doesn't do that for anybody else."

I lay on the cot and held Kenny, patting him on the back. I prayed for him silently and asked the Lord to show me what was wrong with him. Suddenly, at the foot of my cot I saw a creature that was about four and a half feet tall. It was a battleship gray color, and even its teeth, hair, and fingernails were dull gray. It had a vicious, ugly, perverse-looking face.

This creature snarled at the baby and thrust its hand toward Kenny. The fingers of this creature disappeared into Kenny's chest and, when they did, Kenny doubled up in pain. I was shocked when I realized that, in the spirit realm, I was seeing a demonic being. I rose up in bed and threw my hand toward the demon. I rebuked the demonic spirit in the name of Jesus and commanded it to leave the baby alone and to leave the house immediately.

When I spoke those words, the creature backed up three steps and threw his hand out toward the baby. By that time, I was so angry that I was ready to lay the baby down and leap toward this demonic spirit. This creature said to me with a snarl, "I can't torment him while you're here. I can't get back in this house while you're here. But you're going to leave in three days. When you leave, I'll come back in this house and I'll torment this kid and do what I want to with him. And you won't be here to stop me." Then he vanished.

I was furious that a demonic spirit was able to torture my baby brother. All I could do was pray and asked the Lord what could be done to stop this.

During the night I had a dream. God showed me that my parents' lives were unclean. He spoke to me in the dream and said, "While your mother is fixing breakfast in the morning, I want you to tell your parents that I showed you what is wrong with Kenny Edgar. I will not allow this child to be raised up in a sinful environment. I want him to be raised right. I gave your parents this little boy to be a blessing to them and to care for them in their old age. But if they are not going to live for me, I will take him while he is a baby. Tell them that, if they do not repent, I will take this child home to be with me."

You can imagine how shook up I was. I was almost afraid to tell them what the Lord had spoken. Since they were not serving God, I had no idea how they would react. But the next morning during breakfast, I told them what happened the night before, and I told them about the dream and the message the Lord had spoken. "You need to repent now," I told them.

Dad cursed and said, "I can't live for God in this hellhole. Before it's over with, I might kill some of these moonshiners."

Mom said, "Well, Fred, if your dad can't live right, then I know I can't."

And that is the way I had to leave them three days later and go to my next revival.

About two weeks after that incident, I was preaching a revival and staying in the pastor's home. He received a phone call and said to me, "Brother Stone, come to the telephone. Brother McDaniel from War is on the phone and your dad is there at the house. I think it has something to do with your little brother."

Sure enough, it was Dad on the phone, telling me that Kenny Edgar had died. I left the next day for the funeral. We buried him in a homemade casket on the Stone farm in Johnny Cake Hollow.

After Kenny's death, Mom was so distraught that she had a nervous breakdown. Dad suffered a permanent disability, and things became so bad in their lives that they finally realized God was the only solution to their problems. They repented; but by that time, it was too late for Kenny Edgar.

Before Dad became disabled, he had a warning dream. When I went home, Dad said, "Fred, I had a stupid ol' dream last night.'"

I said, "Dad, sometimes God gives me interpretations of dreams. Tell me about it."

He said, "Fred, I dreamed that a great storm with heavy rain and wind hit the farm. It rained and rained. I looked up on the hillside at the orchard, and the wind and rain were cutting big grooves between the trees. Mud and rocks started washing off the hillside. After a while, so much mud and rock came down that it washed part of the foundation of the house away, and it fell over crooked.

"Then, after I dreamed that, I was up in the sky and the same storm was hitting. I looked down and thought, 'Oh, no, I'm going to fall down out of the sky into all of that mud.' A voice spoke to me and said, 'Look down at your feet.' I looked and there was a cloud. It wasn't a big cloud, but it was a solid white cloud. The voice said, 'Step on that cloud by faith. Exercise your faith and you'll be saved.' I stepped out on the cloud and it felt solid under my feet. What in the world does that mean?"

I said, "Dad, the old house represents your body. God is showing you that a terrible illness is going to hit you, and it's going to wear your body down. Certain foundations are going to be destroyed. You may become disabled. The cloud is the gospel and the power of the Holy Spirit. The Lord is telling you that you are going to suffer, but if you will trust God and by faith repent and give your heart to God, He will see you through the difficulty. You aren't going to have anything to hang onto but faith in God. You'd better start praying and seeking God."

Dad had worked in the mines for thirty years and, because of the weight of the tools and materials that he had to carry on his back every day, he suffered with back problems. He didn't know just how severe the problem was until it was too late.

One night during a revival, the Holy Spirit told me, "Go back home. Something is seriously wrong with one of your parents." I had no car at the time, so I left that night and hitchhiked home. I arrived the next day to find that Dad had just been through back surgery and three discs were removed. He was paralyzed from the waist down and in terrible pain.

The surgery left him completely disabled, and he was never able to work in the mines again. For the rest of his life, he was stooped over and barely able to walk. He forced himself to work in the garden to provide food, but it was difficult for him to do even that. Social Security refused to give him disability because they said he was capable of doing light work in the mines. The doctor finally wrote a fiery letter to Social Security and explained that there is no such thing as light work in the mines. They finally gave him disability. In addition to that, twice a year his former coworkers took up a collection and gave Dad the money.

Collectively, those problems helped bring my parents to the Lord. First they lost Kenny. Mom had a nervous breakdown, and Dad was afraid of losing her. Then Dad became disabled. They could do nothing except trust and have faith in God. It's sad to say, but God sometimes has to use tragic events to bring people to Christ. Mom and Dad never thought seriously about their spiritual condition until all of that happened.

After these terrible events, Dad came to the Lord first, in the Bradshaw Church of God during one of my revivals. Shortly after, Mom accepted Christ in a revival. Both were baptized in the Dry Fork River.

One time when I was leaving for a revival, Dad pulled ten dollars out of his pocket and handed it to me. Even though I had no money, I did not want to take his cash because I knew how badly he needed the money. Besides, I had already planned to hitchhike. I said, "No, Dad.

You need that money worse than I do. Keep it; I don't think I should take it."

"No, Fred," he replied. "You need to give me a chance to get a blessing from the Lord. We have kids in school, and your mom and I need a blessing."

That made sense, so I took the money and rode a bus to the revival. Winter was coming and Dad had no income, not even disability at that point. When I came home two weeks later, a truck drove up with eight tons of coal. Dad told them not to unload it because he couldn't pay for it. The driver said, "Mr. Stone, you don't have to pay for this. I have a paid in full ticket for this coal. The ticket says deliver it to you."

Dad said, "What about that, Fred? I gave you ten dollars and I got eighty dollars back!"

For a new believer, that was a wonderful example of stepping out in faith to experience a blessing from God.

CHAPTER 5

Then Came Marriage

In 1954, I was preaching a revival in West Virginia at the Fairmont Church of God where Reverend T. C. Franklin served as pastor. The church was full of young people, but I particularly noticed an attractive, dark haired young woman. She sang with her sister and sometimes her parents sang with them. I asked who she was and learned that her name was Juanita and her parents were John and Lucy Bava.

She could sing and play both the piano and the accordion, so I was very impressed with her musical abilities. A young man named Frank Campbell was dating her sister Janet, and Frank and I became friends during the revival. Sometimes the pastor, Frank, and I visited the Bava home and, before long, Juanita and I started going out to eat together after church.

We lived in different parts of the state, and I was traveling and evangelizing. But if I conducted a revival nearby, her dad drove her to the meeting. I went back to Fairmont to see her every time I had a chance. When I visited their home, we sat on the front porch and I practiced scripture memorization. I had scripture cards, and Juanita gave me the chapter and verse and checked my accuracy as I quoted the scripture.

That was the highlight of our dating. Most of the time, we wrote letters and talked on the phone.

In 1955, eight months after we met, Juanita and I married. Reverend T. C. Franklin performed the ceremony.

I had only a few dollars in my pocket when we got married, so Juanita's dad took me to a finance company downtown and cosigned for me to borrow a hundred and fifty dollars for our honeymoon. I had been depending on money from a revival two weeks earlier, but I came away with almost nothing. During that meeting, a railroad engineer stood up and said, "I don't believe I can afford to keep paying tithes to this church. Drop my name from the membership books." The pastor ordered the clerk to drop his name. Somebody else stood up and said, "I can't afford to pay tithes, either. Drop my name, too." It had a domino effect, with people requesting that their names be dropped after hearing other people make the request. The offering for the entire two week revival was twenty-five dollars.

On borrowed money, Juanita and I went to Davis, West Virginia on our honeymoon. Afterward, we drove to the Church of God State Camp Meeting in Beckley. We didn't have much of anything, and we were driving a Hudson Super 6 automobile that I had purchased from the pastor who performed our wedding ceremony. The car had 150,000 miles on it, and it had already blown three head gaskets. On the way to Camp Meeting, a fourth head gasket blew. I pulled to the side of the road, got out, and raised the hood.

Since this was the first car I had ever owned, Juanita rightly suspected that I knew nothing about cars. She watched as I examined a few things under the hood; then the hood fell and hit me on the back of the head. Juanita thought the whole situation was hilarious, and she started laughing. I don't quite have the same sense of humor, so I walked around to the side of the car and said, "Sister, could you tell me what's so funny?" She said that from that point on, she knew to watch out when I called her "sister."

By the time we arrived in Beckley—and I don't even remember how we got there—it was too late to get a motel room. Juanita's sister, Janet, had gotten married that weekend, and they were staying in Beckley. We went to their motel, knocked on their door, and asked if we could spend the night. They agreed to let us share their motel room on the second night of their honeymoon.

After we got married, we discussed whether we wanted to have children right away. We decided to let the Lord decide. Juanita wanted two girls and two boys, and that is exactly what the Lord gave us. Our daughters are Diana and Melanie, and our sons are Perry, Jr. and Phillip.

———◇———

The year after we married, we were in a revival and staying at the pastor's home. While we were eating breakfast one morning, the pastor asked me, "What town are you from?"

"Bartley," I replied.

"Well," he said. "I see in the newspaper this morning that a man named Spence killed a man named Sammy Williams in Bartley. Did you know those two men?"

I said, "Oh, my goodness! Sammy Williams is my cousin and he lives next door to my Dad." We took a night off from the revival and drove to Bartley the next day to attend the funeral.

When Sammy was a young boy, his mother died from a poisoning. His father remarried but didn't raise him. Sammy lived with my grandparents, the Dunfords, and I believe he always carried anger and resentment because of the situation with his parents. Granddad, being a heavy drinker and a moonshiner, didn't help matters, either.

Uncle Rufus was at the Dunford home one day when Sammy began cursing. Rufus rebuked him and told him that he shouldn't be using that language in front of his grandmother. Sammy grabbed an ax, held it over his head, and threatened Rufus, saying, "I'll split your head open, you Holy Roller!"

Rufus realized the boy had serious problems. He said, "Sammy, you're a teenager and you're old enough to know right from wrong. I'm going to warn you that if you don't repent and turn to God, you could someday die a violent death."

Years went by, and Sammy married and had two children. The family rented a house from Mr. Spence, and Sammy's boy accidentally broke a pane of glass in a window of the house. Mr. Spence became furious. Sammy promised to fix the window as soon as he could, but that didn't satisfy Mr. Spence.

One night about two o'clock in the morning, Mr. Spence came to their home with a loaded gun. He sat it down outside and knocked on the door. Sammy, who was sick and weak with the flu, crawled out of bed and answered the door. The two of them calmly exchanged a few words before Mr. Spence told Sammy that he had a shot for him outside in a fruit jar. A "shot" was mountain terminology for a drink of moonshine liquor. But instead of liquor, Spence was referring to a shot with a shotgun.

Sammy told Mr. Spence that he didn't want to drink anymore because he was trying to give up moonshine. After that simple verbal exchange, Mr. Spence reached for the gun and fired a shot within an inch of Sammy's heart. The bullet when through Sammy's body; then, it went through a sheetrock wall and into the washing machine. He was getting ready to shoot Sammy in the face when his wife and daughter heard the first shot and leaped out of bed.

The daughter, who probably weighed about ninety-five pounds, jumped Spence and grabbed the gun. She pushed him out of the house and cried out, "Why did you shoot my Dad?"

Spence got into his truck and took off. He wrecked a short distance down the road and walked the rest of the way home. He went into the house and confessed to his wife that he had just shot Sammy Williams.

At first Sammy didn't think he was hurt as badly as he was. The family helped him sit down, and one of the children rushed next door to get Dad. He ran to their home and arrived just as Sammy was going into shock. Then he died. Dad almost had a nervous breakdown after Sammy's death. He always cared about Sammy, and he would sometimes come to our home and care for the children when Mom and Dad were gone.

Before this tragedy, I had been witnessing to Sammy. He had already dreamed that he was inside of a mine, and that coal fell on him and crushed him to death. I said to him, "Sammy, the dream means that you are going to die a sudden death. It might even be an argument." He seemed to be concerned and I believe that he wanted to change.

God warned Sammy in a dream of his violent death because He did not want Sammy to die lost without Christ. I believe the Lord will try to warn sinners, giving them an opportunity to turn their hearts to Him before it is too late. But too many times, people harden their hearts and turn in rebellion against God. In doing so, they die lost. Before he died that night, Sammy had time to give his heart to Christ. I hope that he did, but only God knows.

The Bible tells us that righteousness leads to life, but those who pursue evil pursue it to their own death. In our coal mining community, we saw firsthand the truth of that scripture. There was hardly a family in Bartley that was not touched by evil and death.

Juanita and I continued to evangelize for four years, but it was not an easy life for two newlyweds. I recall barely having a dime to my name, and preaching a revival at one church where the pastor did not collect an offering because he was sure that nobody had anything to give. He said, "Anyone got anything to give tonight? I know you haven't. I know you all could barely get here tonight and you don't have anything to give." For that two week revival, I made forty dollars, which wasn't enough to cover the car payment and gas to and from the revival. Pastors would plead for revival, but so many of them seemed to think the evangelist could live on air.

In those days, evangelists were not housed in hotels or special apartments. They stayed in someone's home during the revival, so we never knew where we would be staying or under what conditions. Some people treated us like royalty, while it was clear that others were housing us with great reluctance. Juanita will never forget the time we stayed in a home where the man would not allow her to wash the dishes with detergent because he fed the dish water to the hogs.

Finally the state overseer asked us to temporarily pastor a small church in the southern part of West Virginia until he could find a permanent pastor for the congregation. We agreed to do so. When we arrived, we had nothing to eat. In those days, people occasionally brought food and groceries to the pastor and his family. I have no idea where this term originated, but these collections of food were called "poundings." When we first arrived at this church, Juanita and I decided to pray for a pounding.

She prayed for a steak, and I told the Lord that I wanted cornbread and pinto beans. About an hour later, a man whom we did not know— he even attended another church denomination— came to our house with a basketful of food. Inside the basket we found milk, a bag of pinto beans, canned goods, cornbread mix, and steaks.

But conditions in the parsonage were so bad that we sent our daughter, Diana, to live with Juanita's parents. Juanita could not even fix baby formula because the tap water was so white with sulfur that it was undrinkable. We didn't stay there long, and the state overseer could not find a permanent pastor for the church.

John Bava, my father-in-law, organized a church in Gorman, Maryland and he and I preached the revival that helped to get the church started. Then he helped us organize a new church in Montrose, West Virginia. We rented an old store building which sat about six feet off the main highway and held services downstairs while we lived upstairs. From then on, I continued to serve as a pastor until I retired and we moved to Cleveland, Tennessee.

From the time that the Lord first called me to preach, I have always believed that ministering the gospel of Jesus Christ was the highest calling a person could have. I consider it an honor to have been able to evangelize, pastor congregations, and preach the Word of God. But the ministry has not always been an easy job.

Throughout our ministry, we had to depend on the Lord through many tests and trials. There were times when the churches were not self-supporting and I had to work a full time job to support the family. In some cases, the church could barely pay their utility bills. For the first fifteen years that I served as pastor, I had to work a secular job as well.

When we moved to a small town in Southwestern Virginia, I took a job with the rescue squad. I drove the squad car, took calls, and assisted with first aid care. One morning I received a call from the police department telling me that a Dr. Stevens had tried to commit suicide. At the time of the call, I did not know that this was the same doctor who had once lived in Bartley, West Virginia and had spent several years in prison after being convicted of killing his wife.

I went along on this call and we rushed to the scene. Dr. Stevens had been in his office when he went into a mad rage and stepped on a flower container to ram his fist through a window. Then he stepped off the container, and the broken glass ripped his arm wide open. He was on drugs at the time of the incident.

He ran next door to the barbershop, dressed only in his pants and socks. When the rescue squad arrived, he was sitting in a barbershop chair. His left arm was bleeding profusely because he had sliced an artery on the broken glass. With every heartbeat, his blood shot three feet from the artery.

We tied a tourniquet around his arm, and he ripped it to pieces. The police tried to restrain him as we tied another tourniquet around his arm. The doctor was in such a mad rage that nobody wanted to ride with him in the back of the rescue squad car. At 140 pounds, I was the scrawny one of the bunch. Still, I ended up riding in the back with Dr. Stevens and a police officer named Rollins.

Again, the doctor broke the tourniquet. When I tried to tie another one around his arm, he threatened to kick me out the back of the vehicle. He shook and raved like a maniac. Shouting every profane word you can imagine, he cursed and used God's name in vain, saying, "I don't care if I die! I want to go to hell! I'd like to see what hell's like! I've got a lot of friends in hell! Do you think I'm afraid of hell?"

Officer Rollins said, "Doctor, this man is trying to save your life. If you don't get back on that bed and keep your mouth shut and quit cussing this man, I'll use this blackjack and knock your head off."

Dr. Stevens looked at the officer and knew he meant business. He finally calmed down, which I was thankful for since it was a thirty minute drive to the nearest hospital.

Surprisingly, God used that situation to help us. The church was in debt and couldn't pay their bills; they couldn't even borrow money from the bank. But after this incident, word spread around town about this Church of God pastor who had enough nerve to get in the back of the squad car with this crazy doctor. It gave me some fame in the town, and the next time I went to the bank to cash my fifty dollar paycheck, the banker came out and shook my hand. He said, "Preacher, if you need any money, just come here and we'll get you whatever you need."

Before that time, the bank wouldn't loan us a dime. I was sorry about the medical doctor trying to kill himself, but I was thankful that God used the situation for the church's benefit.

When we first moved to Northern Virginia, the church had experienced some problems before we arrived and the church's membership had dropped to about twelve. The tithe was around a hundred dollars a week. The church could not support a pastor, so Juanita got a job and I helped to build swimming pools with Pete and Harold Dunford, two cousins of mine who lived in the area.

We moved to Northern Virginia during the terrible race and Vietnam anti-war riots of the late 1960s and early 1970s. It was dangerous for anybody—but especially a white person—to drive through the northeast section of the District of Columbia where most of the race riots occurred. But Harold sent me to Maryland one day to pick up supplies. His directions took me through the heart of northeast D.C. where I drove straight into the riots. I seriously thought I would be killed before I got out of that place. When I returned I told him, "You ought to be ashamed of yourself for sending me into D. C! That place was awful! They were rioting, stores were burned, and there was debris all over the streets. People were looking at me like they wanted to kill me!"

He replied, "Well, Fred, I figured I couldn't send any of those sinner boys. They would have been killed for sure. I knew if I sent a child of God, the Lord would have to watch over you."

Sometimes we moved to a new area and barely got unpacked before the problems started. On one occasion, we moved from one state to another to pastor a church. We moved our belongings into the house that was supposed to be the parsonage, only to have a real estate agent knock on the door and ask why we were there. Because of some papers that had not been signed before we arrived, the church congregation was unaware that the house had been placed on the market and sold. We were forced to leave the house immediately because the new owners were expected to arrive from California in three days.

Sometimes the situations were difficult; other times the people were difficult. There were always wonderful people in every church, and we still consider many of them our friends. But I'll admit—and I'm sure many pastors would agree—that the enemy made sure there were always a few troublemakers and chronic complainers in the church. Sometimes the troublemakers came in the form of an entire family. Perhaps it was a family who let me know up front that they didn't vote for me and they didn't want me there. They wanted their Uncle George to pastor this church. They made sure I understood that they ran off the last pastor, and they were going to run me off, too.

In retrospect, I wish I had used more wisdom when I left one church to pastor another. If a church has existed for twenty years or longer and it still has the same forty members and no more, something is wrong in that church. I wish I'd had the wisdom to stay away from some of those churches. And when I pastored a church where the members were good, loving people and the church was growing, I should have had the wisdom to stay. There were two churches that I know I left prematurely.

It was not always easy dealing with difficult church members. But I learned that if a church member won't listen to the shepherd who is in authority over them, the Lord Himself will often use His own strong methods of dealing with these folks.

At one church, a woman stood up during a business meeting, pointed her finger at me, and said, "Come out of him you devil." Thinking that perhaps I misunderstood, I asked her to repeat what she said. And she repeated it.

At that moment, the power of God came over me and I pointed toward her and started speaking in tongues. I had no idea what the Spirit prayed, but the next morning, the woman could not speak. For months she could not speak. She went from doctor to doctor, but none could explain the loss of her voice. As I prayed one day, the Lord said to me, "I am going to heal this woman because her children are crying for her. I am doing it for her children, not for her. She will not repent, and she will not apologize. But if you will pray for her and tell her that you will forgive her for what she said, I will heal the woman."

That is what I did, and the Lord restored her voice. But after that incident, she and her family suffered greatly. Their home burned down twice, she and her husband divorced, and the woman was later killed in a tragic automobile accident. I'm not saying it was her outburst in the church meeting that caused her trouble, but I do believe that she carried a seed of rebellion, anger, and unforgiveness that caused many of her problems.

And sadly, I learned that there are still church members who will try to run you out of town for inviting people of another race to attend your church. In one state that I will not name, I was threatened in my own church by a member of the Ku Klux Klan. One night during a revival service at this same church, two of the church members got into a fist fight in the vestibule. That church was as eager to see me leave as I was to get out of town.

There will always be tests and trials in your life, regardless of your occupation. But the enemy has an especially strong desire to attack those who are working for the Lord. People often believe the pastor has nothing to do except preach a couple of sermons on Sunday. But the pastor's job description includes fighting not just his own battles, but those of everybody in the congregation. The pastor is expected to have all the answers, and sometimes people don't realize that the pastor is human, too. People ought to pray for their pastor just as they pray for their own family.

I learned that I had to stay in close communion with the Lord if I intended to continue working for Him in the ministry. Trust and confidence in God is better than trust and confidence in any other human being, whether it's church officials, a family member, or your best friend. Nobody can hold the place that the Lord Jesus Christ holds. I have experienced this for fifty-six years and I know it to be the truth.

We quickly learned that we had to depend on the Lord for everything. Whatever we wore or ate, God provided it. He was and always has been faithful to supply our needs through His riches in glory. I praise God for His help and His provision through every need.

SECTION TWO
A Flame of Holy Fire

"And it shall come to pass in the last days, says God,
that I will pour out My Spirit on all flesh;
your sons and your daughters shall prophesy.
Your young men shall see visions,
your old men shall dream dreams.
And on My menservants and on My maidservants
I will pour out My Spirit in those days;
and they shall prophesy."

———————————

ACTS 2:17–18

"There are diversities of gifts, but the same Spirit."

———————————

I CORINTHIANS 12:4

CHAPTER 6

Who is the Holy Spirit?

By now, if you are not familiar with the baptism and the gifts of the Holy Spirit, you might have questions about some of the incidents I have related so far. Even within some churches, there are people—including those behind the pulpit—who do not believe that manifestations of the Holy Spirit are real today. *Sure, we read about this in the New Testament,* they say. *But all of this died with the last apostle.*

For those who have a limited knowledge of the Holy Spirit, this is a good place to give an overview. I pray that by the time you finish this book, you will have a full understanding of the Holy Spirit and His purpose, as well as a desire to see Him operate fully in your own life.

Father, Son, and Holy Spirit

The idea of one God existing as Father, Son, and Holy Spirit can be a difficult concept for people to grasp. Some religions teach that Christians worship three separate Gods and are heretics or infidels for believing in the Father, Son, and Holy Spirit.

Deuteronomy 6:4 says, *"Hear, O Israel: The LORD our God, the LORD is one!"* The Hebrew word for one is echad, which ranges in meaning from "one and only one," to "one made up of many." God is one in unity, and the unity of God can be compared to the unity of man. So let's compare the two.

When God created man, He said, "Let us make man in our image. "As part of His image, you have a body, a soul, and a spirit. Your body, soul, and spirit are distinct from each other, but it takes all three to make you a living, breathing human being.

When you die, your spirit and soul will leave your body. The body that your spirit and soul once inhabited will eventually return to the dust of the earth until you receive a new body at the resurrection. Thanks to medical technology and our ability to resuscitate people, we now have contemporary proof that your spirit and soul leave your body at death and go to either heaven or hell. There are people alive today who have experienced and witnessed of this very thing.

Your soul can be defined as your conscious, will, intellect, and emotional being. Think of God—whose knowledge, wisdom, and authority are without limit—as the soul.

Your spirit, which looks like you, will always be alive and well, even after you die. In Luke 23:46, the final words of Jesus before he died on the cross were, "Father, into your hands I commit my spirit." Your spirit can, indeed, exist separately from your body. Most people don't have the experience while they are alive of witnessing their spirit leave their body, but it does happen. I talked about my own experience with this very thing earlier in the book.

Just as you have a spirit, God has a Spirit, whom we call the Holy Spirit. His Spirit is omnipotent, or all-powerful; omniscient, or all-knowing; and omnipresent, or able to be all places at the same time.

The body can be compared to Jesus. He existed in the beginning as the Word, and He later became flesh. *"In the beginning was the Word, the Word was with God, and the Word was God"* (John 1:1). *"Then the Word became flesh and dwelt among us"* (John 1:14). *"He is the Lamb that was slain from the foundation of the world"* (Revelation 13:8). Jesus came to earth as a newborn baby—as flesh to dwell among us. Thirty-three years later, as the sacrificial Lamb of God, Jesus was crucified and buried. Then He rose from the dead and received a new body at His resurrection. Colossians 1:15 calls Christ the image of the invisible God.

A more detailed study could be done on this topic, but for purposes of this book, I will give this brief overview. Do you see the comparison? God created you as a three-dimensional being, just as He is a three-dimensional being. Just like God, you also are one person with a body, a soul, and a spirit.

The Holy Spirit in the Old Testament

Throughout the Bible there are references to the work of the Holy Spirit. His full power was not revealed until the ministry of Jesus, but the Old Testament contains many references to the Spirit of God. For example:

- The Spirit of God existed at the very beginning of creation when He hovered over the face of the water. (Genesis 1:2)

- Pharaoh knew that the Spirit of God was in Joseph. (Genesis 41:38)

- The Spirit of God enabled people to do creative work. (Exodus 31:3-6)

- The Spirit of God came upon seventy elders and anointed them for leadership. On one occasion, the elders even prophesied. Moses said that he wished the Lord would put His Spirit upon everybody, and that all of the Lord's people would be prophets. (Numbers 11: 25 and 29)

- The Spirit of the Lord came upon Othniel, Gideon, Jephthah, and Samson, enabling them to deliver the Israelites and perform miraculous deeds. (Judges 3:10; 6:34; 11:29; 13:25; 14:6, 14:19, 15:14 and 15)

- The Spirit of the Lord came upon Saul, and later David, when they were anointed and equipped to fulfill their destiny. The Spirit of the Lord later departed from Saul, and a distressing spirit troubled him. (1 Samuel 10:6-10; 16:13-14)

- The Holy Spirit sometimes transported Elijah from one place to another. (1 Kings 18:12; 2 Kings 2:16; 2 Kings 2:1-13).

- When Gehazi lied to Naaman and took gifts, Elisha witnessed this in the Spirit. (2 Kings 5:20-27)

- The Spirit of the Lord inspired Azariah, Jahaziel, and Zechariah to speak prophetic utterances. (2 Chronicles 15:1-2; 2 Chronicles 20:14-17; 2 Chronicles 24:20)

- Isaiah prophesied of the baptism of the Holy Spirit and called it refreshing rest for the weary. (Isaiah 28:11-12)

- The Spirit of the Lord fell upon Eziekel and used him to bring prophetic words of judgment. The Spirit of the Lord took him up and brought him in a vision into Chaldea. The Spirit of the Lord set him down in the valley of dry bones. (Ezekiel 11:1-5; Ezekiel 11:24; Ezekiel 37:1)

■ The prophet Joel saw a time in the future when the Spirit of God would be poured out on all flesh. He said that sons and daughters will prophesy, old men will dream dreams, young men will see visions, and the Spirit will be poured out the world over, even upon those who are considered the lowest by societal standards. (Joel 2:28-32)

■ Micah was full of power by the Spirit of the Lord, which anointed and enabled him to prophesy the word of God to wicked rulers and false prophets. (Micah 3:8)

The Spirit of God was active in the Old Testament from the beginning of creation. In these few references are examples of supernatural anointing, words of knowledge, discernment of spirits, miracles, and prophecy. In fact, every Old Testament book from Isaiah to Malachi contains prophecies that were given through the inspiration of the Spirit of God.

The Holy Spirit in the New Testament

You might be familiar with the account of the outpouring of the Holy Spirit in Acts chapter two. But here are some New Testament references to the Holy Spirit that preceded the outpouring in the upper room on the Day of Pentecost:

■ John the Baptist—the son of Elisabeth and Zacharias—was filled with the Holy Spirit, even from his mother's womb. (Luke 1:15)

- Elisabeth and Zacharias were also filled with the Holy Spirit. (Luke 1:41 and 67)

- Jesus was conceived when the Holy Spirit came upon Mary. (Matthew 1:20; Luke 1:35)

- When Jesus was baptized, the Spirit came upon Him in the form of a dove. (Matthew 3:16; John 1:32)

- Jesus, being full of the Spirit, left the Jordan River and was led by the Spirit into the wilderness. (Matthew 4:1; Mark 1:12, Luke 4:1)

- Jesus was tempted by the devil, but the Spirit equipped Him to face the enemy and resist temptation. (Matthew 4:2-11)

Since Jesus was born as an infant and lived on earth as a man, even He had to be supernaturally empowered by the Spirit of God for ministry. Likewise, we need to be supernaturally empowered by the Holy Spirit for our work on earth. Jesus was tempted by the devil; yet through the Holy Spirit, He resisted. Likewise, through the Holy Spirit, we too can face the enemy and resist his temptations.

After Jesus was crucified and buried, the Holy Spirit raised Him from the grave and gave Him a new, resurrected body. Likewise, the Holy Spirit raises us from spiritual death and, when we die physically, He will raise us from the grave and give us a new body at the resurrection.

Another Comforter

Toward the end of Jesus' ministry, He told His disciples that the Father would send the Holy Spirit, not just to dwell *with* them, but to dwell *in* them. The first manifestation of this occurred after the resurrection, when Jesus breathed on His disciples and said, *"Receive the Holy Spirit"* (John 20:22). This was a picture of the breath of life for all believers under the New Covenant. It represents the Holy Spirit that draws us to Christ and comes into our life the moment we accept Jesus as our personal Saviour.

Jesus called the Holy Spirit another Comforter:

"If you love Me, keep my commandments. And I will pray the Father, and He shall give you another Comforter, that He may abide with your forever" (John 14:15-16 KJV).

"But the Comforter, which is the Holy Ghost, whom the Father will send in my name, he shall teach you all things, and bring all things to your remembrance, whatsoever I have said unto you" (John 14:26 KJV).

The Greek word for another is allon, and it means "another of the same kind." Jesus was telling His disciples that the Holy Spirit would be with them at all times to help them do the same work that He did while on earth. Think about this: With the Holy Spirit at work on earth, it would be as though Jesus Himself were here in the flesh ministering alongside them!

The Greek word for comforter is parakletos. Besides comforter, the word also means helper, friend, ally, advocate, advisor, and strengthener. Jesus is also referred to as the parakletos (advocate) in 1 John 2:1: *"My little children, these things I write to you, so that you may sin not. And if anyone sins, we have an Advocate with the Father, Jesus Christ the righteous."*

Jesus is our parakletos in heaven, and the Holy Spirit is our parakletos on earth. Both in heaven and on earth, we have a friend, comforter, helper, ally, advisor, and strengthener.

Before Jesus was crucified, He gave this message to His disciples:

"Most assuredly, I say to you, he who believes in Me, the works that I do he will do also; and greater works than these he will do, because I go to My Father. And whatever you ask in My name, that I will do, that the Father may be glorified in the Son. If you ask anything in My name, I will do it" (John 14:12-14).

"Nevertheless I tell you the truth; it is expedient for you that I go away: for if I go not away, the Comforter will not come unto you; but if I depart, I will send Him unto you" (John 16:7 KJV).

Jesus expects all of us—not just His early church disciples—to do more than He did while He ministered on the earth. One reason this is possible is because, while Jesus lived on earth, He could not be all places at one time. Even though Jesus was a man who was birthed by the Holy Spirit of God, He still had earthly limitations.

When Jesus returned to heaven, God sent the omnipresent Holy Spirit who *can* be all places at one time. The Holy Spirit dwelling *with* us and *in* us gives each of us the same power that enabled Jesus to do great works during His earthly ministry. What an awesome gift this is, to be able to do the same works that Jesus did, as though He were here in the flesh ministering alongside us!

What is the Baptism of the Holy Spirit?

Before Jesus ascended to heaven, He told His followers to wait in Jerusalem for the Promise of the Father. He was referring to the Holy Spirit:

"And being assembled together with them, He commanded them not to depart from Jerusalem, but to wait for the Promise of the Father, 'which', He said, 'you have heard from Me; for John truly baptized with water, but you shall be baptized with the Holy Spirit not many days from now' " (Acts 1:4-5).

"But you shall receive power when the Holy Spirit has come upon you; and you shall be witnesses to Me in Jerusalem, and in all Judea and Samaria, and to the end of the earth" (Acts 1:8).

That is indeed what happened. Jesus ascended into heaven; then His followers received the Promise. In Acts chapter two, we read where 120 of Jesus' followers were waiting in the upper room when a sound came from heaven, like a mighty rushing wind. Divided tongues, like fire, sat upon each one of them, and they were all filled with the Holy Spirit and began to speak with other tongues.

This outpouring in the upper room is considered by most to be the birth of the New Testament church. After that, the church began to experience tremendous growth. Those Spirit-filled believers left the upper room with a burning desire to spread the gospel message of salvation through the shed blood of Jesus Christ, and that is exactly what they did. The first message recorded in the Bible immediately following that outpouring was preached by Peter. This is the same Peter who, not long before, denied that he even knew Jesus. But here he is in Acts chapter three, preaching a sermon that resulted in three thousand people being saved and baptized!

The Holy Spirit enabled Christ's disciples to spread the gospel, perform great miracles, and withstand terrible persecution. No longer were they intimidated by Roman soldiers or anybody else. The Holy

Spirit comforted them and gave them strength to be courageous, even in the face of death. And according to historical accounts in *The New Foxes Book of Martyrs,* nearly all of Christ's early disciples died a martyr's death.

James, the brother of John, was beheaded. His courage so impressed one of his captors that he made a confession of faith and was beheaded along with James. One historian said that James, the brother of Jesus, was stoned, while another said he was thrown from the Temple tower; then his head was smashed with a club. It is believed that Mark was dragged to pieces. Philip, Andrew, Peter, Jude, and Bartholomew were crucified, some after having received a severe beating. Thomas was impaled with spears and thrown into a flaming oven. Paul was beheaded, as were Matthew and Matthias, the disciple who replaced Judas. Historians aren't certain what happened to Luke, but he may have been hung from an olive tree.

The only apostle whom we are certain did not die a violent death was John. However, he was arrested in Ephesus, sent to Rome, and placed into a vessel of boiling oil. When that did not kill him, the Emperor Domitian banished him to the Island of Patmos. While on this island, John documented the visions and prophecies that we read in the book of Revelation. After his release, John returned to Ephesus and died around A.D. 98.

There is no question that it was the power of the Holy Spirit in their lives that helped these men stand courageously and spread the gospel throughout the world, knowing that the penalty would almost certainly be death. And even in death, they stood strong and firm in their faith. They would not be defeated.

Through these great disciples and the infilling of the Holy Spirit in their lives, the gospel spread just as Jesus said it would. His disciples were witnesses to Christ throughout Jerusalem, Judea, Samaria, and other parts of the earth. Those disciples died, but throughout history, others have picked up the torch and carried the message of Christ and the fire of the Holy Spirit around the globe.

Jesus said, "I will build my church, and the gates of hell shall not prevail against it." Indeed, no matter what the enemy has tried to throw against it, the church has prevailed. We have done greater things, just as Jesus said we would. And since that first outpouring on the Day of Pentecost, hundreds of millions of people have accepted Jesus as their personal Savior and been baptized in the Holy Spirit.

That same Promise is still available to every believer today who desires it and asks. Along with the infilling of the Holy Spirit, there are nine gifts of the Spirit that can operate in the life of a believer.

Gifts of the Spirit

The Apostle Paul wrote letters to the church in Corinth, Greece, giving them instruction and counsel on a variety of practical and doctrinal issues within the church. He included information about the gifts of the Holy Spirit:

"Now concerning spiritual gifts, brethren, I do not want you to be ignorant. There are diversities of gifts, but the same Spirit. There are differences of ministries, but the same Lord. And there are diversities of activities, but it is the same God who works all in all. But the manifestation of the Spirit is given to each one for the profit of all: for to one is given the word of

wisdom through the Spirit, to another the word of knowledge through the same Spirit, to another faith by the same Spirit, to another gifts of healings by the same Spirit, to another the working of miracles, to another prophecy, to another discerning of spirits, to another different kinds of tongues, to another the interpretation of tongues. But one and the same Spirit works all these things, distributing to each one individually as He wills" (1 Corinthians 12:1, 4-11).

We see that there are nine gifts of the Holy Spirit:

1. word of wisdom
2. word of knowledge
3. faith
4. gifts of healings
5. working of miracles
6. prophecy
7. discerning of spirits
8. different kinds of tongues
9. interpretation of tongues

Each of these gifts displays the powerful presence of the Holy Spirit of God. They make the Lord more real to both the believer and the unbeliever by providing evidence that there truly is a God, and He still is actively involved in our lives today.

The Holy Spirit convicts us of sin, gives us new life in Christ, enables us to witness for Him, brings the Word of God to life, and teaches us to apply His Word. The gifts of the Spirit build up, sanctify, and empower the church. These nine gifts are distributed to each person individually as the Lord chooses.

Here is a brief explanation of each supernatural gift of the Holy Spirit:

- *Word of wisdom* – a spiritual declaration that applies the Word of God or the wisdom of the Holy Spirit to a specific problem or situation. (This is not the same wisdom that we gain through prayer and the study of God's word.)

- *Word of knowledge* – an inspirational revelation that provides knowledge from God about a specific person or circumstance. It will usually address an immediate need or situation.

- *Faith* – a supernatural ability to trust and believe God for the miraculous. This gift typically operates along with the gifts of healing and miracles.

- *Healing* – every born again believer should pray for the sick. But through the prayers of a believer who operates in the gift of healing, the supernatural power of God will often bring restoration of physical and emotional health to the sick.

- *Miracles* – supernatural acts of God that often change the course of natural law. When God performs a miracle, He does something that could not be done through human effort.

- *Prophecy* – an utterance that comes directly from God by a prompting of the Holy Spirit. It reveals the will of God in a specific situation, and it might offer comfort, edification, exhortation, or even warning or judgment to one or more people in the body of Christ. It can also expose the condition of a person's heart. (This is different from the ministry of a prophet that is spoken of in Ephesians 4:11.)

- *Discerning of spirits* – enables the believer to recognize whether a spirit, a prophecy, a word, or any other manifestation is truly from the Holy Spirit. This gift is extremely important because the Bible warned us that, in the last days, false prophets would come and deceive many. Without this gift, people can be easily deceived.

- *Different (or divers) kinds of tongues* – allows the Spirit-filled believer to supernaturally speak in different languages that are unknown to the speaker. The languages could be ones that are actually spoken on earth, or heavenly languages that are unknown on earth.

- *Interpretation of tongues* – through the Holy Spirit, this gift makes known the meaning of the revelation that was spoken in tongues. The interpretation—which will be a prophecy, word of knowledge, or word of wisdom—is for the believers who are assembled. Those who speak in tongues should pray for the gift of interpretation.

All nine gifts of the Spirit operate according to the will of God. It is carnal and sacrilegious for man to try to control the gifts of the Holy Spirit. God gives and controls these gifts; not man. Some gifts will operate through a believer on a regular basis, and many believers have more than one gift.

The Apostle Paul told us in First Corinthians 12:12-31 that we should not honor one person over another based on their spiritual gifts. Neither should we be intimidated by someone who is used in these gifts. Each person has a purpose within the body of Christ, and each is gifted according to the will of God. The gifts should not be used with pride. They should not be used for personal exaltation. They should be used humbly and with a sincere desire to benefit others.

The baptism and the gifts of the Holy Spirit did not disappear with the death of the last apostle. This is not an experience that existed only in the ancient past. The proof is that, since the outpouring of the Holy Spirit at the Azusa Street revival in 1906, hundreds of millions of people around the world have received the baptism of the Holy Spirit and the gifts that accompany the infilling. This move of the Spirit has not been confined to Pentecostals. Believers of other denominations—Baptists, Methodists, Catholics, Presbyterians, and others—have received this gift, which birthed the Charismatic movement.

The Holy Spirit and His gifts are for everybody who believes. He will never be confined within denominational boundaries.

We Need the Holy Spirit

All of the manifestations of the Holy Spirit in my early Christian life helped prepare the way for my future ministry. Any believer who earnestly and humbly desires to be a vessel for the Holy Spirit can have those same kinds of experiences.

Every believer needs the infilling and the gifts of the Holy Spirit. If the Holy Spirit is not operating in a church, everything becomes a lifeless routine and a dead ritual. We can employ the latest technology and an exceptional worship team. We can install coffee bars and gymnasiums, and provide entertainment by the latest well-known Christian artists.

But if we do not invite the Holy Spirit, the church will lack spiritual life. Church will become nothing more than a place to socialize.

Even Pentecostal and Charismatic leaders should exercise caution that their church services do not become regimented. Pastors and worship leaders must be sensitive to the direction of the Holy Spirit and allow the Lord to disrupt their scheduled services. Let the Holy Spirit move when He wants to move. Don't allow your flesh to usurp the authority of the Spirit of God.

I have sat in services where the Holy Spirit gave a message in tongues and I could sense that the Lord wanted to move mightily in the service. But instead of allowing that to happen, the congregation was led in a lively song, or the offering was collected, or announcements were given. That hinders the Spirit, and He will not continue to move in that kind of environment. The Bible warns us not to quench—that is, hinder—the Holy Spirit.

If we want the presence of the Holy Spirit in our midst, we must learn to let Him move. Be willing to throw aside scheduled agendas and allow God to be in charge of the service. After all, we do not come to church to be entertained. We come to worship and magnify the Lord.

CHAPTER 7

Faith, Healing, and Miracles

From that overview, I will tell you about some of the manifestations of the Holy Spirit that I have seen throughout my life and ministry. First I will talk about the powerful gifts of faith, healing, and miracles. These usually operate together since it takes faith to believe for healing and other miracles from God.

The Gift of Faith

Faith, as a gift of the Spirit, is divinely planted within us; it is not something that we can produce in our own minds or with our own power. The gift of faith gives us supernatural confidence that God can and will answer our prayers. Even the disciples who ministered with Jesus realized they needed great faith, so they asked the Lord to increase their faith (Luke 17:5).

There is a faith teaching which says that if we have a problem, we should not confess it. But practically speaking, it is impossible to deny that we have a problem; instead, we should believe that God is bigger than our problem and declare that He is able to meet our needs.

God wants His people to have faith to minister to those who are in need and to believe that an answer will come. Isaiah 53:4-5 says, *"Surely He has borne our griefs and carried our sorrows; yet we esteemed Him stricken, smitten by God, and afflicted. But He was wounded for our transgressions, He was bruised for our iniquities; the chastisement of our peace was upon Him, and by His stripes we are healed."*

What kind of spiritual dedication do we have to our Saviour who was wounded, bruised, and beaten for us if we allow people to remain sick, oppressed, possessed, or in need of some kind of miracle? What does it say about our love for others when the Lord is willing to deliver them, yet the righteous do nothing?

In James 1:6-8 we read, *"But let him ask in faith, with no doubting, for he who doubts is like a wave of the sea driven and tossed by the wind. For let not that man suppose that he will receive anything from the Lord. He is a double-minded man, unstable in all his ways."*

A double-minded person is drawn in opposite directions. Sometimes he believes; sometimes he does not. Sometimes he thinks God is on his side; sometimes he thinks He's not. A double-minded, unstable person moves with the wind. He will have an inconsistent prayer life, and he might be unstable in other areas of life as well.

We need a stable faith in order to receive anything from the Lord. If you don't believe, you won't receive.

The Gift of Healing

Those who have the gift of faith almost always have the gift of healing to pray for the sick. The promise of healing is found in both the Old Covenant and the New Covenant. In Exodus 15:26 God told His people,

"If you diligently heed the voice of the LORD your God and do what is right in His sight, give ear to His commandments, and keep all His statues, I will put none of the diseases on you which I have brought on the Egyptians. For I am the LORD who heals you."

This is called a covenant of healing because it is a promise from God to heal those who heed His voice, do what is right, and obey His commandments. The Hebrew word for heal is rapha, which means "to cure, heal, repair, mend, and restore health." There is no question that this verse refers to bodily healing.

A New Covenant promise of healing is found in James 5:14-18: *"Is anyone among you sick? Let him call for the elders of the church, and let them pray over him, anointing him with oil in the name of the Lord. And the prayer of faith will save the sick, and the Lord will raise him up…"*

Some people who do not believe in divine healing teach that the oil spoken of in this verse was a medicinal product that was used for healing. If that is true, why aren't we still using that oil today?

But the oil was not medicinal; it was symbolic of anointing the sick with the Holy Spirit. The scripture clearly states that it is the Lord who will raise them up; not the oil. It is also clear from scripture that the prayer of faith will heal the sick.

It is God's desire that we, through prayer and the power of the Holy Spirit, perform miraculous deeds. Miracles glorify the Lord, prove that prayer works, and confirm that the gospel message is true. Miracles include, but are not limited to, divine healing.

When we pray for healing and miracles, we should pray with fervency. James 5:16 says that the effectual, fervent prayer of a righteous man avails much. Effectual prayers are active, energetic, miracle-producing prayers.

Fervent prayers are powerful, passionate, and burning with zeal. They come from the depths of the heart.

There is not space in this book to tell you of all the healings and miracles that I have seen the Lord perform in my lifetime. But here are some things I have experienced that will give you insight into how the Lord works, even today. He is the same yesterday, today, and forever; He is still concerned about every phase of our lives.

When our daughter Diana was four years old, she developed strep throat. The pediatrician gave her a double shot of penicillin, and within a couple of days, Diana became critically ill with scarlet fever and was hospitalized. Her fever was so high that the nurses had to cool her in baths of ice water. Her veins were collapsing, and the nurses had to place intravenous drips in her back, ankles, or anywhere they could detect a vein. I recall a physician who stood over her with his eyes closed, trying to take his fingers and detect a normal vein. None could be found.

Blisters and two-inch long welts formed on her entire body, giving an appearance that her body had been burned. She was losing vital fluids and electrolytes that were almost impossible to replace because there was no way to get them into her body. Her kidneys had stopped functioning. On top of all that, she was allergic to the penicillin and sulfa drugs that she had been given.

The hospital called specialists from the National Institutes of Health to come and check her. The NIH doctors were furious at the medical doctor who had given her the drugs. One of them said, "Mr. Stone, don't call that man a doctor in our presence. He has given this child enough drugs to kill an adult." Her condition worsened until doctors told us that, without a miracle, she would not live past midnight.

During this time, the Church of God was having a minister's meeting in Baltimore, Maryland and my father-in-law, John Bava, told them of the urgent need for a miracle. The ministers prayed and, within the hour, her kidneys started to function again and the Lord began to completely heal her body. Three days later, we took her home. There is no question that her healing was a divine miracle of God.

I had my own unusual experience with healing when I was about thirty-five years old. The problem started when I began to feel that I had been punched underneath my heart. Then I would become so physically weak that I had to lie down and rest. Through an examination, the doctor located a tumor that he said was probably on an adrenal gland . He sent me to the University of Virginia Medical Center in Charlottesville for further tests.

Doctors at the University of Virginia performed medical tests for several days. On the sixth day, as I stood and looked out the window of my room on the fourth floor, I sensed that someone was watching me. I turned around, but the other patient in the room was reading the newspaper, so I knew it wasn't him. When I turned back to look out the window, standing outside in midair, I saw a man! I knew this had to be one of God's angels or some kind of manifestation of the Holy Spirit, because what human could be standing outside a fourth floor window in midair?

This man looked intently at me, from the top of my head down to my feet, as though examining me. Then he took a few steps and walked toward me. He had a spiritual body, and his body walked right through my body. I actually felt his back to my back when he walked through me. This lasted a few seconds, and then he stepped back through the window and once again stood facing me. He looked intently at me one more time before he turned and vanished.

Immediately I felt energy from the top of my head to the bottom of my feet, and it was evident that a supernatural power had touched my body. I left the room and walked down four flights of stairs to the lobby. I walked around the lobby twice; then I bolted back up the stairs to my room. I had so much energy that I ran the stairs, taking three steps at a time. When I got to the fourth floor, I was not even out of breath.

As soon as I started into my room, a nurse told me that I had a phone call from Ohio. It was Juanita's brother-in-law, Frank Campbell, who attended a church in Mentor. When I picked up the phone, Frank asked, "What happened at eight o'clock?"

I told him the story. He said, "At eight o'clock, our pastor read some scripture and started to preach. Then he stopped and asked me to stand. He asked if I had a brother in the ministry who is sick. I told him yes, and that you are in a hospital in Virginia undergoing tests for a tumor. The pastor called me forward and asked some of the men in the church to come forward and pray for me on your behalf. The pastor anointed me with oil and the Spirit of God fell on me and on the entire congregation. I asked the pastor if I could call you, and I'm calling right now from his office in the church."

The next morning, the doctors told me that their previous tests detected deep internal bleeding and they would have to run some tests over again. I told them what happened the night before, even though I was certain they would be skeptical. I stayed for several more days while they ran the tests again, but no sign of any problem could be found. To this day, I have had no trace of a tumor or internal bleeding.

FAITH, HEALING, AND MIRACLES | 125

The Gift of Miracles

Often we think of miracles only as they relate to healing. But a miracle is anything that God does supernaturally to either alter the course of nature or to manifest Himself against the enemy. Through the power of the Holy Spirit, God is able perform all kinds of miracles in every situation of your life.

There are many people who have someone in their family who is bound with a spirit of alcoholism or drug addiction. Often, we complain about someone's behavior, yet we seldom ask the Lord for His anointing to intervene in that person's situation. But when you ask, this is what can happen through your faith, prayer, and obedience.

I was a guest speaker in a church where a woman in the congregation came forward and tearfully requested prayer for her alcoholic husband. He was a good husband and father, and she loved and spoke highly of him otherwise. But she did not want to see him ruin his health through alcoholism.

I asked her to give one hand to me and the other hand to the pastor. We prayed for the anointing of God to come into her hands. Then I told her, "When your husband falls asleep, gently place your hands on his throat and his stomach. We have prayed for the anointing of God to touch his body so that the next time he drinks alcohol, it will make him so sick that he thinks he's going to die. Let's believe together that the Lord is going to make him sick and take away his desire for alcohol."

Two days later she came to church and gave this testimony: "When I arrived home from church the night we prayed, my husband had already passed out from drinking. I did exactly as you told me. As he slept, I laid my hands on his throat and stomach and began to pray. While I was praying, I received the baptism of the Holy Spirit and spoke in tongues. I had to leave the room to keep from waking my husband.

"The next day, he tried to drink a glass of bourbon. In less than five minutes, he was vomiting. He told me, 'There's something wrong with this bourbon.' He opened another bottle, took a drink, and immediately became sick and vomited. He kept saying, 'What's wrong with this bourbon?'

"Finally I confessed. I told him, 'I don't think there's anything wrong with the bourbon. I'll tell you what happened. The pastor and the evangelist prayed for you at church the other night. They said, 'Let an anointing come upon this man so that the next time he drinks liquor, it will make him so sick that he thinks he's going to die. Get this desire for alcohol out of his system. Give him a desire to serve God.'

"He was skeptical, but I told him, 'It happened, didn't it? If you don't believe it, try it again.' "

Another simple, yet miraculous answer to prayer occurred during an altar service when the Holy Spirit revealed that a woman was present who had become antagonistic toward her husband because of his serious and continuous verbal abuse. God revealed that she loved her husband, but she didn't know what to do about his abuse. She had prayed but had not seen any change.

A lady stood and wept as she came to the altar. Then a man left his seat and walked toward the altar. I approached the man and asked him about his need. He said, "That's my wife. Everything that you said through the Holy Spirit is true. I don't know how my wife can stand to live with me. I don't know why I'm so abusive. I'm mean and hateful and I don't know why I treat her the way I do. If she left me today I wouldn't blame her one bit."

I told the man that it took honesty and humility to come before the church and make that confession. This husband and wife knelt together and prayed for God to deliver him from that abusive spirit. The couple had never attended this church before, but the Spirit of the Lord sent them there that night for deliverance. Thanks to the Holy Spirit and a couple's obedience, a great miracle of God occurred in their marriage that night. Often people seek months of counseling, when just one encounter with the Holy Spirit will bring an answer to their problems.

———◇———

I have seen the Lord perform miracles in job situations. God is your provider, and when you are faithful to obey His word and to support His work, He will rebuke the devourer. I have never seen God fail to come through for a faithful servant. Malachi 3:8-10 says that those who rob God in tithes and offerings are cursed. But when you give back to the Lord that which belongs to Him, He will open the windows of heaven and pour out such a blessing that there will not be room enough to receive it.

There was a young man in our church who worked for a tire manufacturer that had been purchased by a Japanese company. The new owner upgraded the manufacturing equipment, and this young man was having a problem learning to use the new equipment. The situation was so bad that he was on the verge of losing his job.

He and his wife were faithful church members who supported the work of God and gave back to the Lord that which belonged to Him.

This young man came to me after church one night and expressed his concern about the job situation. They company had given him until the end of the week to be able to do the work or they were going to fire him.

That night, I held his hands and prayed for coordination—that his eyes and hands would be able to work together to master the equipment. The following Wednesday night, he came to church and told me that on Monday, everything started falling into place and he was able to use the equipment. The Lord knew of this young man's urgent need, and He answered prayer and intervened on his behalf the very next day. From that point on, he never produced another bad tire.

———◇———

The Lord also cares about your unsaved family members. He cares about the lost and dying loved ones that you are holding up in prayer, and He is capable of performing a miracle, even at the last moment, to ensure that they do not die without Christ. First Peter 5:8 tells us to be sober and vigilant, because our adversary, the devil, walks about as a roaring lion, seeking whom he may devour. In times like this, it is important to understand that you have authority through the Holy Spirit to rebuke the devourer.

Early one morning I received a phone call from a woman in our church whose brother was dying of AIDS. Her parents had called to say that this young man was not expected to live past six o'clock in the evening. He was a backslider who, at one time, had been a faithful member of the church but had been drawn into a homosexual lifestyle. When he became critically ill, he was living with another young man.

My church member was very concerned that her brother would die without repenting and giving his heart back to Christ. She asked me to call the hospital and try to talk to him, which I did immediately. His nurse answered the phone, and I told her who I was and the purpose of the call. She told me that the young man was too weak to talk and couldn't even lift the telephone receiver. I asked her to put the phone to his ear and give me at least a minute.

She put the phone to his ear. I explained to this young man that I was his family's pastor, and that I was calling to pray for him. Within seconds, the nurse was back on the phone. She told me that he shook his head no and turned his head away.

This disturbed my spirit, because I knew that the enemy was trying to destroy his life and did not want him to repent and return to Christ before his death. The Holy Spirit spoke to me and said, "Ask the nurse to put the phone to his ear again. This time, rebuke the evil spirit immediately and offer prayer for his salvation. Don't try to have a conversation with him."

I told the nurse that I would appreciate it if she would try again and give me one minute of time. She agreed and put the phone back to his ear. I called the young man's name and said, I rebuke this evil spirit from off your life that has tried to destroy you. In the name of Jesus, I command the power of Satan to be broken completely." Then I prayed a quick prayer for his restoration and salvation. I heard him trying to speak, but I learned that he was not speaking to me. He was praying.

When the nurse got back on the phone, she said, "Pastor, I don't know what just happened, but something broke from off his life. I could see it. A look of hope came on his face and he was trying to pray."

He died around six o'clock that evening. This same nurse told his parents that something good happened to their son before he passed away.

The young man lived in another state and the family tried to find a minister to conduct his funeral. Each person they asked refused to conduct the funeral of someone who died of AIDS. They asked me to do it, and I did. His death occurred in the early years of the AIDS epidemic, and there was much fear at that time about how the disease could be transmitted. The upper part of his casket was sealed in either glass or some type of heavy plastic. And even though there was a large crowd at his funeral, most of the people would not come near the casket.

The enemy tried to destroy this young man's life and, in the natural, he succeeded. But thanks to the power and authority of the Holy Spirit and a sister who cared about him, God intervened and gave him new spiritual life. The young man passed from this life—the one that the enemy destroyed—into eternal life with Jesus Christ. I have no doubt that this young man's family will see him again one day in heaven.

Doubt and Unbelief

One thing I learned firsthand from the ministry of Rufus Dunford was that sometimes it is necessary to ask the Lord to remove our doubt and unbelief. In Luke 17:5, we read where even the disciples had to ask the Lord to increase their faith. These were people who followed Jesus during His ministry, yet they needed more conviction, more confidence, more trust, and more belief!

After a sermon that I preached in Florida, I prayed and asked the Lord to bind my unbelief and increase my faith. I asked the Holy Spirit to have His way in the altar service. About that time, the anointing of God struck me and I said, "God just gave me a revelation. There are people in this service who have had a spiritual dream, and you are troubled by it. You have asked for the interpretation and have not received it. The Lord said that, for the first ten people who come forward, He will give you the interpretation to the dream."

Ten people came forward and told me their dreams. The Holy Spirit gave me the knowledge to reveal the interpretation of every single dream these people had. Each person confirmed that what the Holy Spirit revealed was true. I had never experienced anything like that before and never have since. But that just shows you what the Lord can do when you ask Him to remove your doubt and unbelief.

CHAPTER 8

Different Tongues and Interpretation of Tongues

As a teen-age convert, I was in awe and greatly inspired by the way the Lord spoke through tongues and interpretation. I eagerly looked forward to being in church and hearing someone speak forth a message in tongues, then hearing someone interpret the message.

Some people teach that the gifts of tongues and interpretation are no longer valid today. But both gifts are in the Bible, and nobody has the authority from God to do away with this or any other biblical gift. People can fight the baptism and the gifts all they want, but they cannot change the minds of those who have received these gifts and know the truth.

A Heavenly Prayer Language

When we receive the baptism of the Holy Spirit, we are given a heavenly prayer language that is known only to God. What, you may ask, is the point of praying in an unknown language when we can pray in our natural, known language? The Bible mentions three benefits of a heavenly prayer languge:

- The apostle Paul told us that, when we speak in an unknown tongue, we edify ourselves. In other words, when we pray privately in our heavenly prayer language, we build ourselves up in the Spirit.

- When we don't know what we should pray for, we can pray in the Spirit. He knows how to pray in that situation and will pray for us. When we pray in the Spirit, we are praying not to men, but to God. To our natural ears, we speak mysteries.

- When we pray in our earthly language, we sometimes pray with unbelief. We might not have faith to believe God for an answer. But when the Spirit is praying through us, He does not pray with doubt and unbelief. He knows the perfect will of God, so He prays a prayer of faith that aligns with God's perfect will. The Holy Spirit will never pray a prayer that contradicts the will of God.

Interpretation of Tongues

A private prayer language is for use in your private devotions. But when someone in a public setting speaks forth a message in tongues for the entire congregation to hear, there must be an interpretation (1 Corinthians 14:6-19). There are believers who have received the gift to interpret messages that are given in tongues. Through the gift of interpretation, the entire church will be edified. Without an interpretation, there can be no edification for the assembled body of Christ.

So here you have two situations. First, someone speaks forth a message in an unknown language. Then someone interprets that message. The interpretation of tongues, just like speaking in other tongues, comes directly from God. These two gifts operate independently of each other;

yet, they are from the same Holy Spirit. Those who speak in unknown tongues do not understand what they are saying, but sometimes the Holy Spirit will also give them the interpretation of the words they spoke. According to scripture, those who speak in an unknown tongue should also pray to interpret (1 Corinthians 14:13).

Likewise, the person who speaks forth the interpretation of the message does not, in the natural sense, understand the words that were spoken. But the Holy Spirit gives that believer the interpretation.

Here is an example. Someone who speaks and understands only the English language might speak out a message in a perfect Greek language. Another person who might speak and understand only the English language will be given the interpretation. In the natural, neither person can speak nor understand the Greek language, but the Holy Spirit supernaturally gives them the words to say.

This will be an interpretation, not a word-for-word literal translation. The Holy Spirit will simply explain what the Lord is saying through the message given in tongues. For example, one person might say, "The Lord would say, I will deliver you tonight if you will only believe." Someone else might say, "The Lord says, this night you can receive your deliverance." When the King James Version was the only translation of the Bible that was used, people interpreted messages using 17th century English. They might have said, "Thus saith the Lord, I am the God who delivereth thee. He who believeth this night will be delivered."

Different (Divers) Kinds of Tongues

Earlier in the book, I gave personal examples of the gift of different kinds of tongues. The language of the Holy Spirit can be a heavenly language that is not understood by anybody on earth. But different tongues often represent languages that are unknown to the speaker, yet known and spoken on earth by other nationalities or people groups. Sometimes, in the natural, the language can sound very strange. For example, I heard of someone who spoke a language in tongues that sounded similar to a grunt. Yet a missionary who was present in the audience recognized the sounds as the dialect of a tribe of people to whom he had ministered.

Because languages differ so much, sometimes a message in the Spirit will be short while the interpretation will be long, or visa versa. Since some people do not understand that, they may question why an interpretation varies in length from the message.

Throughout my ministry, I have had many experiences with different kinds of tongues. Sometimes these experiences occurred as I prayed privately for someone who understood the language I was speaking through the Spirit.

In one case, I was at the altar praying for a man in our church who had spent many years working in the Middle East. I started praying in the Holy Spirit and speaking in a language that I did not understand. When I finished praying, the gentleman said to me, "You were praying in a perfect Arabic language. You spoke my name and asked the Lord to fill me with the Holy Spirit." I did not know the Arabic language, but later I learned that this man spoke seven languages and Arabic was one of them. He understood everything the Spirit was saying while I prayed for him.

In a similar incident, a medical doctor and his wife who were members of a large Methodist church in Washington, D.C. occasionally visited our church. His wife was of German descent and, one Sunday, she came to the altar and requested prayer for healing. She did not specify what her problem was.

As I prayed for her, I began to speak in the German language. In the natural, I can neither speak nor understand German. But through the gift of different tongues, the Holy Spirit prayed through me in that language. When I finished the prayer, this lady said, "You just prayed the most beautiful prayer for me in the German language. My dad doesn't speak German any better than you do. And you prayed for exactly what is bothering me."

The Lord also healed her completely. Even though this couple was not familiar with Pentecostal worship and the baptism of the Holy Spirit before they visited our church, this prayer and her healing encouraged both of them in their faith. They began to attend our church regularly, and both were an outstanding blessing to the church.

A Sign to Unbelievers

Paul told us that tongues could be a sign to an unbeliever by revealing the secrets of the unbeliever's heart, convicting of sin, and proving that God is in your midst (1 Corinthians 14:20-25). Here is one example of that. An abusive Greek immigrant, who was strongly opposed to his wife attending church services, stood outside the door of a small church building one day and planned to come inside and force his wife to leave the service.

But a Spirit-filled man inside the church stood up and—not knowing that this Greek man was outside the door—faced the door and put his hands up. The Holy Spirit came upon him and he spoke in Greek. He said, "The Lord God of Israel says, I have seen your violent spirit. I have seen your hatred toward my work. Unless you repent, your soul will be lost and in hell."

The Greek man on the other side of the door was so shocked that he ran into the church and came straight to the altar and repented. He confessed to the congregation that he had not believed in any of this and had even cursed it. He admitted that he had come to the church to forcibly remove his wife from the service. Yet after hearing this message that was spoken in tongues while he stood outside the door of the church, this unbeliever was convinced that God is real.

In another unusual incident, I was sitting in a service where my son, Perry, was preaching. The service was being telecast live on satellite around the world.

In the middle of his sermon, the Spirit of the Lord came upon Perry and he spoke a brief message in another language. Through the Holy Spirit, I understood everything that he spoke. I stood to give the interpretation. But the Lord stopped me and told me to let Perry continue his sermon because the message had been heard by the person who needed to receive it.

I will not mention the man's name that was spoken in that message, but the Lord specifically called someone's name. And He said to this man, "This is the Lord God of Israel, the God of the prophets and patriarchs, speaking through my servant. You have been taught death, darkness, and destruction. If you continue in this, you and all of your generation will perish from the earth."

Later I talked with a Christian from Pakistan and inquired about the identity of the man whose name had been spoken by the Holy Spirit. He told me that this individual was the son of the leader of a predominately

Muslim country. There is no question that this man was watching Perry's sermon on satellite television, and the Lord used the gift of different tongues to send him a message in the middle of an American minister's sermon. If that is not a sign to an unbeliever, then tell me what is!

CHAPTER 9

Prophecy, Word of Wisdom, and Word of Knowledge

The gifts of prophecy, word of wisdom, and word of knowledge operate in a similar fashion, so they are often grouped together. These gifts are given to the Spirit-filled believer so that the thoughts and knowledge that are in the mind of God can be revealed to His children.

The Gift of Prophecy

In 1 Corinthians 14:1, the apostle Paul said, *"Pursue love, and desire spiritual gifts, but especially that you may prophesy."* In this context, the word desire means "to be zealous for, to pursue ardently, to desire eagerly or intensely." Paul spent the previous chapter telling us that we should first have love because, without love, we are like sounding brass and clanging cymbals. Without love, we are nothing.

When we first have love for people—those both inside and outside the body of Christ—the gift of prophecy can operate through us to edify, strengthen, exhort, encourage, and comfort believers. The gift of prophecy will build up the believer and reveal the thoughts of God. Prophecy operates under the will of God; not the will of man. A true prophetic word comes as God initiates it, not as man initiates it. Every prophetic word must be judged according to the Bible; that is, it cannot contradict the written Word of God.

When I say that God can give prophetic words to Spirit-filled believers, I am not talking about self-appointed prophets. I'm talking about humble, sincere, praying, Holy Spirit-filled believers in Christ who are truly used of God.

In the Bible, a true prophet was someone who received and proclaimed a message from God. That is still true today. The Lord speaks through the Holy Spirit, and the person who has been given the message serves as God's spokesperson. Just as in biblical days, there is such a thing as a false prophet.

Here are two examples of the operation of prophecy in the Old Testament. Nathan confronted David about his hidden sin and David repented (2 Samuel 12:1-15). In another instance, Isaiah told Hezekiah that he would die. When Hezekiah prayed to the Lord and asked for mercy, God told Isaiah to tell Hezekiah that He heard his prayers and saw his tears, and was going to add fifteen years to his life. Not only that, God was going to deliver the city from the hand of the Assyrian king (Isaiah 38:1-6).

One example of prophecy in the New Testament was when Agabus told Paul that, when he went to Jerusalem, the Jews would bind him and hand him over to the Gentiles (Acts 21:10-12). The Lord had already been dealing with Paul about that, and the message that Agabus spoke simply confirmed what Paul already knew in his spirit.

Those are biblical examples of personal prophecies, or words that the Holy Spirit prompts one person to give to another. This gift can easily be abused by people who are operating in the flesh or attempting to control others. Many people have been hurt by so-called prophetic words that did not come by revelation of the Holy Spirit.

Here are some guidelines to follow when you receive a personal prophecy:

- Examine the character of the person giving the prophecy. Is the individual known to be godly and trustworthy?

- Was the prophecy given by someone who often tries to manipulate and control your actions or the actions of others? If so, it is wise to consider that the prophetic word might not be credible.

- Does the prophecy confirm something the Lord has already been dealing with you about? When you receive a word from someone, you will either have a quickening in your Spirit that the word is true, or you will receive additional confirmation of that word in the future.

- Does the prophecy line up with the Bible, the written Word of God?

- Do not act immediately on any prophetic word that you receive, especially if it does not confirm what the Lord is already telling you. Always weigh it out and pray about it before you take action.

- Once you receive confirmation from the Lord, then you should take action. Keep in mind that prophetic words do not always happen automatically. For example, if you have a confirmed word that the Lord is going to use you in ministry, you cannot expect the Lord to make it happen while you sit in front of the television.

Many times, I have seen the Holy Spirit intervene prophetically to comfort and encourage God's people. For example, sometimes they have lost their jobs through no fault of their own, and the Lord quickly brought an answer through a prophetic word.

I recall one service where I had already preached and was ready to dismiss. But before I could do so, the Holy Spirit gave a message similar to this: "Thus says the Lord God to my servant: Very shortly, your faith will be shaken. Apprehension and fear will come upon you. But do not worry and fret about it, for soon I will bless you greater than you ever have been blessed."

The next day, a church member who had worked for the same company for eighteen years and could have retired with a pension in seven years was dismissed from his job. The company had been purchased and they fired many of the workers. The gentleman called me and said, "Now we know what the Holy Spirit's message was about."

"Did you take the message by faith?" I asked him.

"Yes, I did," he replied.

"Do you know what you're supposed to do?"

"Yes," he said. "I'm taking a few days vacation to relax and enjoy myself. Then I'm going out next Monday to look for a job."

That very Monday, he found a more enjoyable and better paying job. The Lord did, indeed, bless him more than he had ever been blessed.

In another job-related situation, a church member came to me and told me how distressed he was about the financial wrongdoing of his employer. After a disagreement over the situation, he quit the job because, as a Christian, he refused to work for somebody who was dishonest.

The gentleman came to my office and said, "When I make the payment on my trailer this Tuesday, I'll have ten dollars left. I need another job."

He and I prayed, and that night I had a dream. A man walked up to me in the dream and stood to my right. I did not see his face, but he gave me directions to a gas station and said to me, "Call this man's house and tell him to be dressed at 8:00 tomorrow morning. Tell him to go to this gas station, walk inside, and say to the man inside the station, 'I heard that you are in need of an employee.' "

It was about 1:00 in the morning, but I got out of bed and called my church member's house. His wife wrote down the information.

The next week the gentleman told me, "I did what you said. When 8:00 came, I got in my car and drove off. I followed the directions you gave me and went to the station. I was so nervous that I was almost shaking. I walked in and told the man that I heard he might need a fellow to work for him.

"The man said, 'Well, it all depends, buddy. I've had a few men working for me and they were stealing me blind. I've been asking God to send me a good, honest Christian man. Are you an honest Christian man?'

"I said to him, 'I sure am. The pastor of my church called me last night and said the Lord told him to tell me to come here and ask you about a job.' The owner asked me how soon I could go to work, and I said, 'I'm ready right now.' "

Both of these men were faithful to God and to His work through the church. In both situations, God supernaturally intervened when they lost their jobs. He rebuked the devourer. He protected those who were faithful heirs of salvation. The Lord will defeat the plans of the enemy against His people. Humble yourself before God and seek His face. He has promised to bless and provide for you.

Word of Wisdom

The word of wisdom is a supernatural revelation given to us through the Holy Spirit of God. Since God has infinite wisdom, He has all the facts before Him that ever have been and ever will be. He would not be the Almighty God if this were not true.

Today, just as we see throughout scripture, God's divine wisdom is supernaturally conveyed through several means: His audible voice, angelic visitations, dreams and visions, and spoken revelation. This kind of wisdom is not acquired through educational means. It does not come through deep spiritual understanding of the scriptures. It is not the wisdom of man. It is simply a revelation from God and a gift for all believers.

Through divine revelation, a word of wisdom can bring an answer to a problem that you, the church, or even the nation are facing. Through the Holy Spirit, you receive the revelation and know exactly what to do in your difficult circumstances. God can even give you a divine revelation of a business that you should start. It might be something that you would have never thought of on your own, perhaps a creative idea or invention.

When we first moved to Northern Virginia, the church had experienced problems before our arrival, and about twenty people were in attendance that first Sunday. Juanita and I were both working secular jobs, but our car needed mechanical work and we had no money.

One evening, I felt led of the Lord—not through a voice, but through pressure—to buy some art supplies and canvas. I had never painted in my life and had no experience or talent, as far as I knew. But one evening

I painted a picture of Monument Valley from a magazine photograph that was slightly larger than a postage stamp. The Lord supernaturally gave me instructions as I went along. Within a few hours, I had painted an eight by ten oil canvas, which I sold for fifty dollars. I painted a few more and sold those. Even though I painted for only a short time, God gave me talent to help when we needed extra money. He will provide for your needs in miraculous ways if you will only trust Him and obey.

The Holy Spirit will give you wisdom to get out of a dangerous situation if you remain sensitive to His voice throughout the day and are willing to listen and obey when He speaks. Here is a personal example of how the Lord used a word of knowledge and divine wisdom to protect me.

Years ago, I was traveling alone on the interstate highway when I stopped at a rest stop. The only other vehicle in the parking lot was a van. As I got out of the car and locked the door, the Holy Spirit spoke to me and said, "There are three hippies in that van. When you go inside, they are going to severely beat you and rob you. Get back in your car."

I snapped my fingers as though I forgot something and walked back to unlock my door. I reached over and put the key in the ignition; then I got inside the car, locked the door, and started the ignition. The moment I did, three hippies jumped out of the van and rushed toward my car. I floored the accelerator and, as far as I know, they all jumped safely out of my way.

What would have happened to me had I ignored the warning and brushed it off as my imagination? How many times have people suffered because they ignored the Holy Spirit when He tried to warn them?

A similar example of divine protection through a word from the Holy Spirit occurred with an elderly Christian woman who lived in an unsafe neighborhood. A man who was high on drugs broke into her house one night. She was terrified and didn't know what to do, but she knew how to pray. The Holy Spirit said to her, "Pretend you are having a heart attack." That is what she did, and it frightened the man so badly that he ran from the house. That sudden word of wisdom might have saved her life.

———◇———

Here is an example of how a word of wisdom kept me out of trouble in the very early years of my ministry. I needed a car and had been looking for one to purchase. I was preaching a revival, and a man who attended the church had two sons who had just arrived from California. They brought along a really nice automobile that they wanted to sell. It looked like a collector's car, and their asking price was far below the actual value.

The boys were eager to get rid of the car. Their father approached me and said, "You asked the Lord to provide you with a car. My sons brought this car from California and they want to sell it. You can get it real cheap, and I think you ought to buy it."

The price was right, so I planned to go to the bank the following day and get the money to buy this great automobile. But during the night, I had a dream in which the Holy Spirit told me to turn to a verse in Proverbs. In the dream, I did as He instructed. This verse spoke about a person signing a note to borrow money for something that was not legitimate. I asked the Lord to tell me what that meant and He said,

"The Holy Spirit has revealed that you are planning to get a loan for this car, but there is something wrong. You will lose the car and have to pay back the money."

The father of these two boys was upset when he learned that I decided not to buy the car. But it wasn't long before two police officers knocked on the door of the father's house. They confiscated the car, which his sons had stolen, and arrested the boys and took them back to California.

Had I purchased that car, I would have been forced to pay for a stolen car that soon would have been confiscated. Furthermore, I would have had the embarrassment of owning a stolen car. That taught me a lesson: The Lord will protect His children from financial ruin if we will only listen to His voice and be obedient.

Word of Knowledge

The word of knowledge is a revelation by the Holy Spirit of certain facts that are in the mind of God. This can be a revelation into the hidden realm of God's future plans and purposes. Again, God has divine knowledge of everything, and He will convey His knowledge to Spirit-filled believers.

In the Old Testament, Elisha prophetically knew the location of the Syrian camp and was able to relay the very words that the king of Syria spoke in his bedroom (2 Kings 6:8-12). The Spirit revealed Gehazi's dishonesty to Elisha (2 Kings 5:20-27). The Spirit revealed corruption in the church when Ananias and Sapphira stole money (Acts 5:1-11).

A word of knowledge can confirm your destiny. It can bring assurance of coming deliverance or give a promise of future blessings. It can offer guidance in the face of difficult circumstances. The word of knowledge will clean up the church and defeat the plans of the enemy. It can even heal you of self-imposed guilt and bring peace into your life.

After preaching a message one night, I was getting ready to call people to come forward for specific prayer needs. Suddenly the Holy Spirit told me that there was a man in the congregation who had once been forced to shoot another man. The shooting was not this man's fault, but he had been living for years with guilt and condemnation. I spoke this revelation to the congregation and asked the man to come forward for prayer.

A state trooper came forward with his wife and told me what happened years before. During a routine traffic stop, the driver of the car attempted to take the officer's gun and, in the ensuing struggle, the officer fired the weapon and killed the motorist. The officer felt terrible about the killing. He had even received death threats from the motorist's family.

The congregation and I prayed for this man, and the Lord performed an emotional healing in his life. Through the Holy Spirit, obedience, and prayer, the Lord broke a mental stronghold that the trooper had carried for years.

In another church, the Holy Spirit revealed to me through a dream that a member of my congregation was dealing with a similar situation of guilt. This gentleman had served as a United States government agent and, in this dream, the Lord showed me another man who was working as a double agent for both the United States and the Soviet Union. The two had met for a discussion when my friend was attacked by this double agent in vicious hand-to-hand fighting. My friend won the fight by killing the Soviet agent. The Lord even revealed in the dream exactly how the agent was killed.

In the dream, I knew that the gentleman in my church had suffered feelings of guilt for many years over this double agent's death. But the Lord told me to give him this message: The Soviet agent had been ordered to kill you. The killing of this agent was not premeditated and was absolutely necessary to save your own life. You had to do it to survive. I (the Lord) want you to forgive yourself and let it go.

I spoke with this gentleman after church one night, and he wept as he said to me, "Brother Stone, I have lived with this for years. I have never told anybody about that killing so I know that had to come directly from the Lord. Thank you for being obedient."

Both of these men were carrying guilt from situations that occurred in years past. The enemy wanted them to live with condemnation to keep them from walking in the fullness of Christ. But the Lord revealed the situations through a word of knowledge so that the men could release the guilt and be set free from a mental stronghold of the enemy.

———◇———

One time the Holy Spirit revealed information that protected a church member from blackmail. In a dream one night, the Lord showed me that this man who owned a business was going to be blackmailed into reducing his bid on a job. A stockbroker was going to set up a situation involving a Korean woman in an attempt to entrap him.

In the dream, I saw the inside of a restaurant. A man walked in with two attractive Korean women. This man, a stockbroker, sat down at a table with the women, and the businessman from my church walked in and took a seat at their table. They ate dinner; then the stockbroker stood up to leave and one of the Korean women stood to leave with him. The other woman remained seated, and the stockbroker asked my church member to take that woman back to her apartment. The gentleman in my church didn't want to do it, and he told the man to take her there himself.

In the dream, the stockbroker said, "You're supposed to be a Christian and a gentleman. I would think you wouldn't mind doing that." Then he walked out. The Spirit of the Lord told me that this stockbroker had planned to have my church member take this woman home, and the woman was to invite him into her apartment and close the door. The stockbroker knew that this gentleman would not stay in the apartment, but if he could get him inside the door, he could blackmail him.

This dinner meeting was going to happen on Thursday. Through a dream, God was using me to warn my church member so that he could be aware of the situation. The Lord also told me to tell this gentleman to keep his contract price firm. The contract offer was reasonable, and he would suffer financially if he reduced it.

This dream occurred on a Saturday night, and I told the gentleman about the dream the next day after church. One week later, he came to church and told me about an incident the previous Thursday that happened exactly the way the Lord revealed. He told me, "The stockbroker got up and left with one of the Korean women and told me to drive the other woman home. I drove her three blocks away to her apartment, where I opened the car door and told her goodbye. She said that she was afraid and wanted me to walk her to the door. I told her that I had to get home to my wife. She pleaded with me, almost crying, to walk her to the front door. I told her that I was going to stand beside my car and give her three minutes to get inside her apartment. After that, I was driving off. She walked to the apartment by herself."

Through a dream and a word of knowledge, the Lord not only protected this man's reputation, but gave him the contract at his asking price.

--------&--------

Here is another situation where the Lord supernaturally intervened in a financial dilemma. One Saturday night I dreamed that a church member did not have the money to pay eight hundred dollars in property taxes. In this dream, I saw him go to his downstairs family room, kneel before a large, round table, and touch something underneath the table. When he did, a compartment opened. He removed some gold and silver coins and looked at them.

I heard a voice say, "He bought these coins when he worked in Saudi Arabia, and he has forgotten about them. Tell him to pick two gold coins and take them to Georgetown coin dealers. I have prepared a dealer to give him exactly what he needs for the coins."

The next day after the Sunday morning service, I told him about the dream. It surprised him but he said to me, "I had forgotten about those coins. But it's true that I do have them. The table that you saw in the dream was handcrafted in the Middle East, and I watched the craftsmen make that secret compartment. Nobody else knows about that compartment or the coins in that drawer."

He followed the Lord's instructions and took two gold coins to Georgetown. The first dealer offered him less than he needed, so he went to a second dealer. Again, the dealer offered him less than he needed. Because the Lord had promised to give him the amount of money he needed, he accepted neither offer and went to a third dealer. This dealer looked at the coins and said, "I'll give you eight hundred dollars—not a penny more, not a penny less."

What a blessing to know that, through a revelation of the Holy Spirit, the Lord will provide for your needs in such miraculous ways! In all my years of serving God, I have never seen the Lord fail to provide for His obedient and faithful servants.

A word of knowledge will not always bring positive and uplifting news. Even so, the Lord will give His people that knowledge and information for their own personal benefit and protection.

One time during an altar service, the Lord told me to call a woman and her husband forward. She was about eight months pregnant, and I told her that the Lord wanted me to pray for her. As I prayed, the Holy Spirit spoke through me and gave this message: "Very soon your husband is going to leave for work. Within one hour after he leaves home, you are going to start hemorrhaging. Do not hesitate, even five minutes. You must call the rescue squad and go to the hospital immediately. You are going to lose the baby."

Her husband said, "I didn't want to say anything, but I already had a dream that you're going to lose the baby."

The events happened exactly the way the Holy Spirit said they would. When this couple asked the doctor if they could see their baby, the doctor replied, "You don't want to see your baby. Take our word for it." Apparently there was something so terribly wrong with the child that the hospital even had the baby placed in a sealed casket so the body could not be viewed.

A further note to an already sad story is that, after the death of the child, this couple had to deal with a few people in the church telling them that the miscarriage happened because I planted the thought in her mind. That was ridiculous, of course. In His mercy, the Lord was simply warning both her husband and me so that they would be prepared for the situation. Had the Lord not given her detailed instructions, she might have given birth to the child at home and perhaps even hemorrhaged to death.

———◇———

Sometimes the Lord, through a word of knowledge, will reveal something that a person would rather keep hidden. He might reveal an ongoing sin or give a warning to avoid certain temptations. Just like King David and the prophet Nathan, the Lord will give these words of knowledge to expose hidden sin and bring a person to humble repentance.

In one situation, a man held a leadership position in our church when the Lord revealed to me that he was having an affair with a neighbor's wife. The Holy Spirit said to me, "This man is an adulterer. He is in a backslidden condition. You must remove him from his position in the church."

I talked to the man and he confessed that he was, indeed, having an affair. He resigned from his position and left the church. It was sad to see him choose the affair over the Lord, but I could not leave this man in a position of authority in the church after the Holy Spirit revealed his sin and spiritual condition.

People sometimes refuse to listen when they are faced with fleshly temptations. I recall one time that I had asked the congregation to stand for the dismissal prayer when the Lord gave me an instant vision. I saw the wife of a man in our church as she sat at her desk at work. In the vision, I saw in great detail the man who was sitting in front of her in the office. I could describe the wallpaper and paneling in the office. The Holy Spirit warned that this woman would have a spiritual failure if she continued working in that office. I was told to warn her to quit her job immediately for her own spiritual protection.

The woman, who was married with children, ignored the advice and had a serious moral failure with this man which caused the breakup of her home. When the Holy Spirit reveals hidden details of your life and gives you a warning, it is very important to listen and obey.

CHAPTER 10

Discerning of Spirits

Discerning of spirits is a revelation gift that shows by divine inspiration of the Holy Spirit the source of any spirit within an individual, or the source of any supernatural manifestation. Is the manifestation from God? Is it demonic? Is the person operating in the flesh in an attempt to manipulate?

A Spirit-filled believer might be praying for someone and, through the gift of discernment, the Holy Spirit will reveal the types of evil spirits that are controlling the person. Through the gift of discernment, it is possible to walk up the aisle of a church and discern the spirits that are within the church, or within people who are sitting in the church. This gift will also help you discern perverted and heretical teaching. Discerning of spirits is for the protection of both you and the church.

This is an important spiritual gift because demonic spirits can deceive people. A biblical example of this is found in Jeremiah chapter 28. Hananiah prophesied that the yoke would be broken from the king of Babylon, and that all the vessels of the Lord's house that Nebuchadnezzar carried away would be returned within two years. He prophesied that the captives of Judah would be brought back.

But the Lord told Jeremiah, "Go tell Hananiah that the Lord has not sent him. Tell him that he makes the people trust in a lie. I will cast him from the face of the earth. This year he will die because he has taught rebellion again the Lord."

Sure enough, Hananiah died. In Old Testament days, that is what happened to false prophets.

Deceiving Spirits and Doctrines of Demons

The apostle Paul was warned of things that would happen to the church in the future. For instance, in Acts 20:29-30, Paul passed this word on to the church: *"For I know this, that after my departure savage wolves will come in among you, not sparing the flock. Also from among yourselves men will rise up, speaking perverse things, to draw away the disciples after themselves. Therefore watch, and remember that for three years I did not cease to warn everyone night and day with tears."*

In First Timothy 4:1-3, Paul warned the church about apostasy. He said, *"The Spirit expressly says that in latter times some will depart from faith, giving heed to deceiving (seducing) spirits and doctrines of demons, speaking lies in hypocrisy, having their own conscience seared with a hot iron, forbidding to marry and commanding to abstain from foods which God created to be received with thanksgiving by those who believe and know the truth."*

One of the reasons you need the gift of spiritual discernment is so that you can discern false doctrine. A serious problem facing the church today is the amount of strange and deceptive theology that is spreading throughout the church world. We see ministers who claim to be Spirit-filled Pentecostals and Evangelicals who no longer preach against sin because they fear that it might scare people away from their church. Some even teach that there is no hell and that every person on earth is going to heaven. They form new church movements that combine Christianity with New Age practices. And some ministers refuse to say publicly that salvation comes only through Jesus Christ and the confession of your sins.

These ministers have ignored the Bible, twisted the scripture, and developed their own perverse theology. And people have accepted their theology because they have given heed to deceiving spirits and doctrines of demons. A minister who teaches that kind of false doctrine is leading people to an eternity in hell. The blood of those sinners will be on the hands of that minister. It is sad to say, but there will be many ministers whose hands will drip with the blood of lost souls.

Ask yourself: Who are the savage wolves in sheep's clothing that are drawing people away from the truth of the gospel? Does their theology line up with the Word of God? Can their doctrine be proven with scripture? Is their theology just their concept of what the gospel would be if they rewrote it? And how will you know if you don't read the Bible and ask God for discernment?

Evil Spirits in the Church

The church can even be infiltrated by witches and occultists. People who have been involved in the occult and later accepted Christ have told stories of how they once attempted to destroy churches. They attended a service for the sole purpose of calling forth demonic spirits to disrupt the spiritual atmosphere of the church. But those churches that were operating in the fullness of the Holy Spirit frightened them. They claim that they could put a curse on people who were phony, but they could never curse those who were filled with the power of God.

Many Christians choose to remain ignorant of the devices of the enemy, preferring to believe that such things do not happen. Yet there is an example of this in Daniel chapter ten. When Daniel prayed, there were demonic spirits in the atmosphere that blocked his prayer. It took twenty-one days to bring an answer because a chief angel had to fight the demonic prince of Persia before the answer could come.

I believe there is an angel assigned to protect God's churches, but I also believe there is a spirit that the enemy assigns to destroy every church. This is why it is important for the church to walk in love and in the fruits and gifts of the Holy Spirit. The enemy will have a harder time disrupting a church that has that kind of power. And with the gift of discernment, those who are Spirit-filled will spot deceptiveness and evil spirits right away. The Holy Spirit will also give them wisdom to deal with it in a godly manner.

With the many problems that a pastor must deal with in the church, it is important to have the gift of spiritual discernment. Your church will be mightier for the Lord when you operate in that gift. And, in some instances, your church might barely survive unless you can discern and fight the spirits that are hindering your church.

I accompanied my son, Perry, to a revival in a city in Ohio. Unknown to me, the pastor had been fighting severe battles with the enemy as he tried to get a spiritual breakthrough in his church. He had even considered leaving the church. During the first night of the revival, I was on the platform when, during praise and worship, I felt impressed to look toward the balcony. When I did, I saw a fierce and arrogant-looking principality spirit that was sitting on the rail of the balcony. He was smirking and making fun of the people as they worshipped.

The Holy Spirit said to me, "Describe to the pastor what you have just seen. Tell him this is the principality spirit that has been hindering his church for so long. Tell him that I want him to point at the evil spirit and rebuke it with all of his faith and anointing."

When I told the pastor, he thrust his hands toward the balcony, and he and I together commanded this principality to leave the church and never step foot back in the building again. Immediately the spiritual hindrance in the atmosphere broke, and the power of God fell across the building. A revival spirit hit the church and it began to grow mightily. It wasn't long before the church moved into a larger building.

Angels on Assignment

The Lord will also show you the spiritual angel that He assigns to your church to help you in difficult circumstances. I saw one of these angels during a service at a church where I served as pastor. My head was bowed in prayer when God gave me a vision. I saw an angel come down through the roof of the church and stand mid-air in the right hand corner of the building. He had a sword, which he placed in front of himself and held over the church congregation. The Holy Spirit revealed that it was an angel of judgment.

About that time I had begun to experience problems with three people in the church. One was an elderly man who had developed a critical spirit. One was a man who, I regret to say, was drifting away from the Lord, while another man was being used by the enemy to cause dissention.

After I saw the angel with the sword, it wasn't long before the elderly man was knocked down in his home by an invisible hand. He fell onto a radiator and had to be hospitalized from his injuries. When I walked into the hospital room to see him, he and his wife were arguing. She was saying, "You know I didn't shove you into that radiator. I was in the sewing room!"

This was a good man, but he was falling into error. The Lord allowed this angel to bring a judgment against him to straighten him up so that he wouldn't continue to rail against churches and pastors. It worked. After that incident, he was a good, humble man of God and I didn't have any more trouble from him.

The other two men suddenly had to move out of state. All of this happened within a matter of weeks. After that, the Spirit of the Lord began to move in the church in a greater manner.

Hypocrites Behind the Pulpit

It is sad to say, but sometimes you need the gift of spiritual discernment to know what is going on with the person behind the pulpit. Without that gift, it is easy to be deceived.

When my son Perry was about thirteen years old, we were in a church service together. Before the evangelist ended his sermon, I said to Perry, "The Lord revealed something to me about this minister and, for some reason, He wants me to tell you. The Holy Spirit said to me, 'Son, this evangelist is being deceptive with some spiritual gifts. He is going to ask everybody to stand and bow their heads in prayer. He is going to ask them to place their hand on the part of their body where they are suffering. Then he is going to walk down the aisle and call out three people who have placed their hands on various parts of their body and ask them to come forward.' "

Perry said, "Dad, you shouldn't say anything like that."

"No, Perry," I told him. "This is not coming from me. The Holy Spirit just revealed that because He wanted me to tell you."

After the man finished preaching, he did exactly as the Spirit had said. He asked people to bow their heads and pray, and to place their hands on the part of their body where they were experiencing problems. He then walked down the aisle and picked out three people, saying, "Brother, you have a back problem. Come forward. Sister, you have a stomach problem. Brother, you have a heart problem. Come forward."

Perry was shocked. "How did you know that?"

I replied, "I didn't know it, but the Lord did. Evidently the man has developed a technique of claiming to discern things, and it is not being revealed by the Holy Spirit. The Lord is not pleased with what this man is doing. When the Holy Spirit reveals sickness, you can have your eyes closed and your head bowed, and God can speak to you. When the Holy Spirit is operating, you don't need gimmicks.

I recall another time when the Holy Spirit revealed a problem with an evangelist. I was the pastor of a church in a small town when an evangelist who was known by many in this town came to conduct a tent revival. One of our church members knew this evangelist, and the evangelist knew that this woman had a gift of interpretation of tongues. In fact, the Lord had gifted her to interpret any message that was given in tongues.

This church member was visiting our home one day when the Holy Spirit said, "I want you to warn her of a statement someone is going to make that will negatively affect her spiritual life. Tell her that she is going to attend this tent revival tonight. At 8:00 p.m., the music director will give the service to the evangelist. He will go to the podium and instantly appear to give a message in tongues. She will not be able to interpret this message because it will not be anointed. He will try to give the message a second time, and she still will not be able to interpret it because it will not be a message that is given under a Holy Spirit anointing.

"The evangelist is going to be upset that nobody can interpret his message, and he will call her to the front. He is going to prophesy to her that she has cancer. But tell her that I said she does not have cancer."

I repeated to her what the Holy Spirit had said. Since she knew this evangelist, she could hardly believe that he would do such a thing.

I went to the service that night because I wanted to see what would happen with my own eyes. It happened exactly as the Holy Spirit warned. When this evangelist told the lady that she had cancer, she was able to simply ignore it. Through the Holy Spirit, God protected her from the fear and depression that would have come from hearing that she had cancer. We should praise God that He loves His children enough to warn them of such things!

Decades later I reminded her of that "prophecy." She told me, "Brother Stone, I have hardly been sick a day in my life, let alone cancer."

Perverting God's Spirit and Grace

It is carnal and sacrilegious to do as this evangelist did and speak forth a message that did not come from God. He is not pleased with that kind of behavior. If I did something like that, I would fear that God would take this gift from me. I refuse to take that chance because I want the Holy Spirit in my life. I need His guidance every day of my life.

Sometimes people seem to think they can live any way they choose and still be used by God and enter heaven. Not so. In Matthew 7:21-23, Jesus tells us that not everyone who says, "Lord, Lord" will enter into the kingdom of heaven. Only those who do the will of the Father in heaven will enter. Many will claim to have prophesied, cast out demons, and done wonders in His name. But the Lord will be forced to tell them, "Depart from me. I never had a relationship with you."

In his book, *Heaven's Golden Vessel,* Bishop Curtis "Earthquake" Kelley tells of how he died from a brain aneurism and went to heaven until the Lord sent him back to finish his work on earth. While he was in heaven, the Lord told him to go back and tell the church to repent of their sins, including the sins they think are hidden. Those sins included lust, fornication, adultery, witchcraft in the church, rebellion, unforgiveness, lying, and hatred of each other because of the color of their skin. The Lord said that many people believe they can live a sinful lifestyle and enter His holy city, but they will not. He said to Bishop, "Tell them to pray; pray from the depths of their heart. Tell them to fast and seek my face with all of their hearts."

The Lord also told him that ministers who do not repent of their adultery and homosexual lifestyles will die in their pulpits. He states that he knew several such ministers who did just that.

Do not, under any circumstances, sit in a church and listen to a minister who perverts the Holy Spirit and the grace and mercy of God. Ask the Lord for the spirit of discernment to see those things, and get away from that church as quickly as you can.

Oppressed, Afflicted, and Tormented

The gift of spiritual discernment will help deliver the oppressed, the afflicted, and the tormented. Human minds are often driven by cruel, tormenting spirits. In Mark 5:1-8 and Luke 9:37-42, tormenting spirits caused a person to perform acts of violence and self-destruction. Tormenting spirits can cause people to attempt suicide. In Acts 5:16, the apostles prayed for those who were tormented with unclean spirits and the people were healed.

Just as in New Testament times, spirits of dumbness can rob people of their ability to speak. Spirits of blindness can rob people of their sight. Spirits of deafness can rob people of their ability to hear. In Luke 13:11-13, a spirit of infirmity caused a woman to be crippled. Not all physical problems are caused by the presence of evil spirits and spirits of infirmity, but the scripture makes it clear that some are. These spirits can cause physical, spiritual, mental, or emotional weaknesses.

Mental disorders, including schizophrenia, have been healed by the discernment of spirits and prayers of deliverance. Demonic possession—the occupation of a person's body by evil spirits—can be revealed by spiritual discernment. Demons will not yield to human methods, but they will yield to the name of Jesus. In Mark 3:23, Jesus said that Satan does not cast out Satan. Evil spirits will yield only to servants of God and the name of Jesus. The seven sons of Sceva tried it and they were overpowered, wounded, and stripped naked by the very spirits they were trying to cast out.

Around 1971, I received a phone call from my sister, Juanita, telling me that Dad was having a mental breakdown. He was angry and talking nonsense, and he wouldn't eat, drink, or sleep. He had to be watched constantly, or he would go outside and stand in the road. Everybody was exhausted from watching over him, and she asked that I come and help care for him.

I rushed to West Virginia. When I walked in the house, I was shocked at Dad's disheveled appearance and his violent conduct and speech. As soon as he saw me, he began to hit and kick me, while cursing God and using all kinds of profanity. He shouted at me, "You old holy man. I didn't ask you to come to this house."

This went on both day and night for two days. On the third day, I called my brother Lewis and asked him to come to West Virginia to help me with Dad. After he arrived the next morning, I was so exhausted that I fell across the bed and immediately went to sleep. Lewis planned to watch over Dad for a few hours but, in less than an hour, he woke me and said, "Fred, I've never felt anything this horrible in all my life. I was in the Tet offensive and I didn't feel anything that was worse than what is in this house. I am so exhausted that I can't keep my eyes open. You're going to have to get up and watch Dad. I can't take this."

No sooner had I gotten off the bed and stood up than Lewis fell across the bed and went to asleep. I walked back into the kitchen and found Dad raving. I was still praying for his healing, but God was going to show me in a few hours that it was not healing that he needed. It was deliverance.

After Lewis had slept several hours, he woke up and tried once again to take care of Dad. I walked into the same bedroom and fell asleep, completely exhausted. While I slept, God gave me a spiritual dream. I saw Dad's house and he was inside. Eight evil men were inside the house shoving Dad around, pushing him, and trying to knock him off his feet. Dad was suffering terribly from their mistreatment. I was standing outside looking through a window while seeing and hearing all of this. In the dream, I said, "Oh, God, why are these evil men allowed to torment Dad like this? Why are you permitting this?"

Suddenly there were two angels standing to my right side in the dream. One had a package of dynamite in his right hand. The other had a ball of fire in his right hand. The one with the dynamite threw the package at the open chimney, and it hit the edge of the chimney and bounced back to the ground. He picked it up again very carefully and, taking a better aim, he threw it once more. This time, it went through the chimney and hit the floor inside the house. The evil men stared at it but didn't seem to fear it.

Immediately the angel with the ball of fire in his right hand looked at the chimney and swung his arm in an arc. The ball of fire went down the chimney and landed on top of the dynamite. The dynamite exploded into a very hot fire, shooting in every direction toward the evil men. As it shot out, it hit them on their face, their body, their arms, and their hands. The men were terrified as they began to curse and scream. Some fled out the windows, some out the door, and some through the ceiling. Within a moment, the house was completely cleared of these evil men.

Then the Holy Spirit spoke to me and said, "Son, you have prayed for healing. Your Dad does not need healing. He needs deliverance from evil spirits. I am going to give him fifteen seconds of sanity. I am going to restrain the evil powers for fifteen seconds. Watch his eyes and when sanity comes, you will see it in his eyes. He will recognize you and call your name."

When I woke from the dream, I went into the kitchen and sat at the table for several minutes, watching Dad and listening to him continually curse and swear at both me and God. Suddenly the Spirit said, "Stand up. Look into his eyes. I'm going to give him fifteen seconds of sanity. The forces of darkness will be restrained. Act quickly when you see this."

Immediately Dad's eyes became normal. I said, "Dad, who is this?"

He replied in a pitiful tone of voice, "Oh, Fred, something's been trying to kill me. I've been living in pure hell for days."

I said, "Dad, I'm going to lay hands on you and cast out these evil spirits. While I do this, try to say, 'Jesus.'"

He spoke the word Jesus as both of my hands touched his head. The power of God locked onto some kind of demonic power and I jerked my hands off his head. His head snapped back and I felt evil spirits leave through his head. I continued to pray, using the name of Jesus, and once again laid hands on his head. The power of God seemed to grab more evil spirits, and the Spirit of God jerked my hands off his head again. This happened four times. The fourth time, as I felt evil spirits leave his body, Dad became very weak. When he was no longer under the control of these evil spirits, he started to fall to the floor; I grabbed a chair and sat him on it. I kept praising God for his deliverance.

I don't know why Dad succumbed to these evil spirits. But I do know that he was spiritually weak and had no strong Christians around to pray with him or keep him grounded in the Word of God. He had no car and was not physically able to walk miles to church. He had never asked the Lord for the baptism of the Holy Spirit. Somehow, in his weakened physical and spiritual condition, he was successfully attacked by the many evil spirits that were in the atmosphere of that region.

In the situation with Dad, it was not Dad who was saying and doing those terrible things. Dad himself would not have done or said anything like that. It was the spirits within him that were doing this. Demonic spirits must use people to do their evil work. And once they inhabit a person's body, they can destroy the person and everybody around them if the evil spirits are not cast out in Jesus' name. A believer has the power, through the name of Jesus, to cast out these evil spirits and bring healing to the individual.

Do we love God and our fellow man enough to fast, pray, humble ourselves, and seek these gifts that will help us liberate the people who are suffering from these tormenting spirits?

What Spiritual Discernment is Not

People with true spiritual discernment will not be looking for demons in every person and around every corner. Spiritual discernment does not give you the freedom to prejudge, develop a critical spirit, or become a heresy-hunter.

Discernment of spirits is not intuition or keen mental perception. It is not crystal ball or psychic mind reading. People who are involved in that type of activity are responding to the will of man, and their insight is demonic in origin. Demonic spirits can also deceive people by imitating the dead, so don't be fooled by psychics who claim to be able to communicate with your dead relatives.

The Bible warns us that there are counterfeits—spirits of demons that can also perform signs and deceive people (2 Thessalonians 2:9-10 and Revelation 16:14). Recall, for example, the magicians in Exodus chapter seven who were able to imitate the plagues of Moses and Aaron. Spiritual discernment simply helps you know the difference between things that are of God and things that are of Satan or the flesh.

CHAPTER 11

Warnings of Trouble to Come

Job 5:7 tells us that man is born to trouble. In the original Hebrew text, the word "trouble" covers almost any problem we might encounter. It is defined as sorrow, labor, toil, grief, pain, misery, fatigue, and exhaustion. Job also tells us that the Lord will deliver us from our troubles (Job 5:19-21). We will all have our share of trouble in this life; the Bible says so and the enemy will see to it. But when the Holy Spirit is operating in your life, He will warn you of coming trouble, and the Lord is able to deliver you out of those situations.

The apostle Paul was warned by the Holy Spirit not to go to Jerusalem. *"And see, now I go bound in the spirit to Jerusalem, not knowing the things that will happen to me there, except that the Holy Spirit testifies in every city, saying that chains and tribulation await me"* (Acts 20:22-23). Since God knows all things past, present and future, the Holy Spirit could see ahead of Paul and warned him of problems that he would face. Paul went to Jerusalem anyway and, sure enough, he was arrested.

The Holy Spirit will warn of future judgment and guide people accordingly. In the Old Testament, Abraham was warned of future judgment against Sodom and Gomorrah. In the New Testament, Mary and Joseph were warned to go to Egypt and stay there so that Jesus would not be killed by Herod. The wise men were warned not to return to Herod, so they took another route.

The Holy Spirit still warns God's people today. He will warn us of church problems, marriage problems, family problems, temptations, troubles, and even simple everyday problems that a Christian will encounter. John 16:13 says, *"When He, the Spirit of truth, has come, He will guide you into all truth, for He will not speak on His own authority, but whatever He hears He will speak; and He will tell you things to come."*

That verse refers to the Holy Spirit leading you into the full truth of scripture. But I believe it also refers to a Holy Spirit guidance system that protects, leads, guides, and teaches.

God has not left His people to the mercy of the world. He is not going to throw up His hands in defeat while the devil whips you. Through the gifts of the Holy Spirit, God reveals future plans to believers who will listen to and obey His voice. God is no respecter of persons. He will grant these gifts to a statesman like Daniel, to a child like Samuel, or to an imprisoned slave like Joseph.

When you stay in close, daily communion with God, He will warn you of things to come. Pay attention to the voice of the Lord and to the burdens He places on your heart.

Sometimes We Listen and Sometimes We Don't

One of my first warnings from the Holy Spirit occurred in 1952. While driving through English, West Virginia, the Holy Spirit warned me of an impending automobile accident. As I approached a narrow, single-lane bridge, I felt a divine presence in the car and heard an audible voice say,

"Son, slow the car down. The tie rod is getting ready to fall off this car." The voice was so real that I thought perhaps someone had gotten in the car while I was stopped. I turned to look in the back seat and on the floor. Nobody was there.

A second time the voice said, "Son, slow this car down. A tie rod is going to fall off while you are crossing the bridge." The voice spoke yet a third time. I slowed the car down to about ten miles per hour and crossed the bridge. About three-quarters of the way across, I heard a noise as something dropped to the ground. Sure enough, there I sat in the middle of the bridge—unharmed, but with a broken tie rod and no ability to steer the car.

Since the early years of my Christian life and ministry, the Holy Spirit has warned me many times of future trouble and conflict. But there was one time that I did not obey, and we suffered terrible consequences.

In the early 1960s, Juanita, Perry, and I were traveling near Elkins, West Virginia. I was driving about fifty-five miles per hour and had just crossed over a hill a few miles outside of Elkins. As we crested the hill, I saw a car in our lane that appeared to be stopped, yet I saw no brake lights. Thinking that perhaps he was driving slowly, I made a quick decision to pass him. As I started to pass, a truck crested the hill in the opposite lane, preventing me from passing the car. The only thing I could do was stay in my lane and slam on the brakes.

The driver of the car in front of us had stopped in the middle of the road to pick up hitchhikers, and our car skidded into the back of him. There were no seat belts in those days, and Juanita's head went through the windshield. My head cracked the window, and my neck hit the steering wheel with such force that the wheel bent. My voice was never quite the same after that, but it was a miracle that I had any voice at all. Perry—who was about two years old at the time—had been standing up in the middle of the front seat. Moments before the accident, I made him sit down. Thankfully, the impact threw him into the floor instead of through the window.

God miraculously spared all of our lives that day, but that did not stop me from complaining to Him about the accident. I said, "Lord, you know that we don't have the time or the money to be in this hospital. Why did you allow this wreck to happen?"

The Lord spoke to me and said, "I tried to stop you three times, but you didn't pay attention." I thought back, and indeed He had. As I was driving down the road about fifteen minutes before the accident, a deer came out of the woods and stood directly in front of our car. He was blocking the lane and looking straight at us as if to prevent the car from moving forward. I became impatient and drove around the deer.

The second attempt occurred about three miles down the road when we were coming upon an alternate route. I sensed in my spirit that I should get off the main highway and take this route.

As I gave a signal to make the turn, Juanita said, "Where are you going?"

I replied, "I'm taking this shortcut."

"Don't go that way. The road is in terrible condition," she told me.

Again, the Holy Spirit impressed me to take that road, but I did not listen. Moments later we were involved in the accident.

Had I not become impatient when the deer stepped into our path, and had I paid attention to the promptings of the Holy Spirit, we would have avoided that accident. This was one of those lessons I had to learn the hard way. From then on, I tried to always listen and be obedient to the warning voice of the Holy Spirit.

Protection for Family Members

Many times the Holy Spirit has warned me of trouble that is coming upon members of my family. From personal experience, I can tell you that when you receive the warning, take heed and immediately obey the directions of the Lord. Someone's life could be spared by your actions.

This also applies to your family members who are serving in the military. The Lord knows every critical situation they will face in the future, and it is important that you pray for their protection and be obedient to warnings from the Lord. Here is an example of how the Holy Spirit can intervene and protect them from danger.

In 1968, my brother Lewis was a young soldier serving as a Marine in Vietnam when the Holy Spirit warned me that he would face great danger. One night I had just turned off the lights and gone to bed. As I lay there, I saw a bright light at the window. Since that side of the parsonage faced an alley, I knew there was nothing outside that could cause such a bright light. I went to the window and pulled the shade back, and sure enough, it was completely dark outside.

I thought that was odd, but suddenly the Holy Spirit spoke and said, "Be still before the Lord. Lie back down. Your brother Lewis will face great danger." I lay my head back on the pillow and closed my eyes. Just like a television in my head, I saw and heard a raging battle. I heard gunfire and mortar explosions. Darkness was coming on the earth. Marines had formed a perimeter of protection and dug a trench for the night. Some were trying to rest while others stood guard.

In this vision, a Marine guard walked from the left end of the trench to the right. As he walked, I saw three long snakes crawl from one end and drop into the trench. Two of the snakes had rifles strapped on their backs and the third had a knife. I saw the guard in the darkness as he carefully watched and paced back and forth. These snakes spread out several feet apart and waited for the guard to come back to the other end of the trench. I knew that these snakes were waiting to kill this guard.

The Holy Spirit said to me, "Write to Lewis at once. Draw a map and warn him of what is to take place. If you don't do this, his blood will be on your hands."

I did exactly as the Holy Spirit said. About four weeks later I received a reply. Lewis wrote, "Fred, your dream was a true one. We had fought all day and were ordered to dig in for the night. While we were still digging, your letter was in my pocket. Something warned me, 'This is the time and place of Fred's letter.' Instantly shots rang out. I kicked myself off my feet and fell backward. One of my buddies was killed by rifle fire. If it hadn't been for your warning letter, I would have been killed."

Because of the warning of the Holy Spirit and prayers for his safety, my brother Lewis survived Vietnam and is still living today.

Lewis had another close call in Vietnam when he and several other Marines were on patrol, watching for Vietcong guerilla fighters along the Mekong River. He heard a noise in the water and, not far from where he was hidden, a tank with a periscope came out of the water. Terrified, he stayed frozen in that spot.

After the tank passed, he left his hiding spot to report back to the troops. Suddenly, just a few feet in front of him stood a Vietcong fighter who was armed with an AK-47. Lewis and he both lifted their guns and pointed them at each other. Lewis could have killed the man, but the man also would have killed Lewis. They found themselves in a standoff, with each man pointing at the other and neither willing to take the first shot.

Then, very slowly, with his eyes still on Lewis, the Vietcong fighter squatted down as he held the rifle across his open hands. When he laid his weapon on the ground, Lewis did the same. They signaled each other that they did not want to kill each other. The Vietnamese man turned and ran, leaving his weapon on the ground. Lewis picked up his rifle and ran back to his fellow Marines.

Several years after the war ended, Lewis was living in Northern Virginia and noticed that his mail carrier was a Vietnamese man. He walked up to the mail carrier one day to get his mail and immediately recognized the man as someone he had seen before. Lewis said, "I know you from somewhere. Have I met you before?"

After looking at the man for a few moments, Lewis said, "I remember where it was. We met in face to face combat in Vietnam. We could have shot each other but we didn't."

The Vietnamese man reached out his hand and thanked Lewis for not shooting him. Lewis did the same. The man said to Lewis, "I never wanted to fight for the Vietcong, but they forced me to fight. I wanted to come to the United States. At the close of the war, I was able to come. I am thankful to be in the United States."

Thanks to the Almighty God, an incident that could have turned into a tragedy for both men ultimately became a blessing to both.

The Spirit of God will warn you of attacks and problems that will occur every day of your life. When that happens, you must either act on the word at that very moment, or immediately pray about it. When He gives you the revelation, you will know at that moment what action you should take.

Here is an instance when a revelation of the Holy Spirit required immediate action. Our family was traveling along the interstate in separate cars when we were caught in a terrible storm with heavy rain and high winds. Visibility was low, so we pulled to the side of the road to wait for the rain to subside. I was driving the car in front, and Juanita was driving the car behind me. We had been sitting on the shoulder of the highway for a while, when suddenly the Holy Spirit warned me that a tree was going to fall on Juanita's car. I immediately pulled onto the highway and she followed. No sooner had she driven off than a tree fell in the spot where the car had been sitting.

The Enemy Wants to Attack the Children

Most of us are concerned for the safety and welfare of our families—especially our children and grandchildren. Through the Holy Spirit, the Lord will warn you of destruction that the enemy has planned against your children. The enemy will especially try to attack those children who seem to have a call of God on their lives at a young age, and he will attack your children who are actively involved in doing the Lord's work.

Another reason why the enemy wants to destroy our children is because of the word spoken by Joel, who prophesied that in the last days, God's Spirit would be poured out on all flesh, and sons and daughters would prophesy (Joel 2:28). The more sons and daughters that Satan can kill or keep in sin and bondage, the fewer sons and daughters there will be to prophesy the words of the Lord in the last days.

I think of the young Muslims who become martyrs and suicide bombers. My heart grieves when I see these handsome young men who were created to enjoy life to an old age. God wanted them to marry and have children. He wanted them to live to see their grandchildren. But their lives have been snuffed out by an enemy who taught them that the pathway to paradise was through death, darkness, and destruction. Now they are in hell for eternity, and there is no turning back.

Only through fervent prayers, especially those of parents and grandparents, can our children be protected from the evil plans of the enemy.

My son Phillip and I were in Israel in 1986 when the Holy Spirit gave me a warning that he was going to face a problem in the days ahead. In the Spirit, I saw him sitting on an airplane; beneath the seat, fire was trying to reach his body. It could not reach him, but it was trying. I prayed and earnestly asked that, whatever this trial was, the Lord would watch over and protect him.

Soon after we returned home I received a phone call from a surgeon, asking our permission to do emergency surgery. Phillip had developed severe abdominal pain and had driven himself to the hospital. His gallbladder had burst before he arrived, and the doctor said that he was in critical condition because of the poison that had entered his system. The warning and subsequent prayer might have saved his life.

The Holy Spirit has given me several warnings for my son, Perry. One night the Lord woke me up after midnight with a terrible burden. I knew that Perry was driving out of the Washington, D. C. area after a church service, and I knew this burden was for him. I prayed fervently for his protection.

Perry left the church that night and began the five-hour trip back to Salem, Virginia. While driving, he fell asleep on the interstate highway with his cruise control set. Something—most likely an angel sent from God—touched him and he woke abruptly. He turned the steering wheel just in time to miss hitting a concrete bridge abutment. Again, the Holy Spirit gave me a burden that night to pray, and I believe those prayers protected him.

Another warning occurred when Perry and one of his friends took a trip to Crater Lake, Oregon. They were on the back side of a volcano when Perry decided to explore the volcano. Keith, the friend who accompanied him on the trip, refused to go along because he feared that it was too dangerous. So Perry went alone. That was not one of his brighter moments.

As Perry walked along the back of this inactive volcano, the volcanic rock loosened and he, along with the rock, began sliding down the side of the volcano. There was nothing he could grab onto to break his slide since everything was loose volcanic rock. At the bottom edge of the volcano was Crater Lake, which is nearly two thousand feet deep in some places.

Meanwhile, I was on the east coast, driving down the highway with Juanita and our daughter, Melanie. Suddenly I had a strong burden to pray for Perry. I stopped the car, let Juanita drive, and got in the back seat of the car to pray. The Holy Spirit told me that he was in grave danger and to intercede for him.

While Perry was on the west coast falling down the side of a volcano, I was on the east coast in the back seat of the car praying for him. Back at the volcano, a long, sturdy stick appeared from out of nowhere. Perry sensed that if he hoped to survive, he needed to grab the stick and use it to dig himself to safety.

I strongly believe that the enemy, in one of his schemes against a child of God, planted a thought in Perry's mind, giving him an irresistible desire to walk the back of that volcano. If Perry had thought about the danger or stopped to pray about it first, he certainly would not have done such a thing. In this case, God knew that it was too late to speak to Perry. So He allowed the Holy Spirit to place a burden upon me and tell me the great danger that he was in.

A third warning occurred after we moved to Cleveland, Tennessee. I had been fasting for three days and on the third day, in the middle of the afternoon, the Lord gave me a full color vision. I saw two demonic beings, one stronger and physically larger than the other. The larger one was screaming and raging at the smaller one and saying, "Why did you allow him to get that information about us?"

The smaller demonic being said, "I don't know how he got it. I watched him day and night to make sure he didn't get the information. I did everything to sidetrack him. I don't know how he got it."

The larger power said, "He has the information and he's publishing it. If he goes forward with this and does much to harm us, I will kill him."

It came to me in the Spirit that these demons were talking about Perry. This was during the time that the Holy Spirit was giving Perry several unusual revelations, and he was preaching things that people had not traditionally heard. One of those revelations was about the role that Islam will play in the days of the antichrist.

Indeed, the enemy did make several unsuccessful attempts on his life the following year. But through three days of fasting, the Lord prepared me to see into the demonic spirit realm and actually listen to the plans of the enemy so that I could warn Perry in advance. Furthermore, I believe it was the prayers of his intercessors, led by a prayer warrior named Bea Ogle, which thwarted the plans of the enemy on his life.

Protection for the Backslider

A person who has never accepted Christ or has backslidden from the Lord does not have a covenant of protection with Him. But through your own covenant with the Lord, your prayers can sometimes protect even your lost loved ones.

We were living in North Carolina when the Holy Spirit warned me of an incident involving my brother Morgan, who had been living in a backslidden condition for many years. One afternoon, I was in the parsonage, lying across my son Phillip's bed and reading the Bible. Suddenly I heard footsteps to my right side and thought perhaps it was Juanita. Instead, the right hand of a man—I knew it was an angel—reached out and touched me on the top of my head. Instantly, I was having a vision.

In the vision, I was standing about fifty feet in the air on a highway near Iaeger, West Virginia. I saw a terrible accident involving a coal truck and a small pickup truck. A loaded, 30-ton coal truck had rounded a curve and crossed about four feet over the center line. The coal truck hit the pickup truck head-on, smashing the entire cab all the way to the truck bed. Inside were the driver and another passenger. The passenger was my brother, Morgan. His head had been smashed and was hanging in pieces, while arteries were spurting blood from his neck. The driver was also crushed under the steering wheel and fatally injured.

The Holy Spirit said to me, "This is your brother, Morgan. Today he will be killed by a coal truck between the hours of three and four o'clock p.m. unless you intercede for him.

It was already a few minutes before three o'clock, so I jumped off the bed, grabbed the church keys, and told Juanita not to allow anybody to disturb me. I rushed next door to the church to pray.

I prayed from three to five o'clock p.m. The intercession was so stressful that I actually suffered bodily pain while I was praying. It felt like I was wrestling with death itself for Morgan's soul. While I was praying the Lord spoke to me and said, "Son, I've tried many times through your prayers to reach Morgan, but he won't listen to me. He has willfully turned his back on me and is not following me. He is not in covenant with me and he will not listen to my voice."

I cried out to God, "Why did you tell me to intercede for him? If you can't reach him, then what am I praying for?"

The Holy Spirit spoke, "Do you remember years ago when I told you that I would give you two angels to help you in times of urgent need? Pray for one of those angels to go and protect Morgan."

I remembered those angels because the Lord showed them to me when I was a pastor in Northern Virginia. He told me that the angels would not always be with me, but that when I was in urgent need, to call and they would be sent to assist me.

Immediately I pleaded, over and over, for the Lord to send an angel to protect Morgan. I prayed until I felt a release and the burden lifted. That two-hour experience left me physically exhausted.

I went back to the house and called Morgan. It was about 5:15 p.m. when he answered the phone. I said, "Morgan, don't say anything until I tell you what happened. I've just finished an intercessory prayer for you. Satan was planning your death on the highway today. You would have been killed between the hours of three and four o'clock. A coal truck would have hit you head-on while you were in your pick-up truck."

I described the scene as I saw it in the vision and told him that both he and his driver were killed. I said, "Morgan, you are not ready to die. You are away from God, and He had me interceding for you to keep you out of hell."

Morgan's voice quivered and, finally, he was able to speak. He said, "Fred, it happened exactly like you said. We were driving toward Davy. Suddenly a thought came into my mind and I said to my buddy who was driving, 'Pull over at this place. I need to talk to Alan Ball.' We stopped and went inside. After I got inside, I couldn't remember why I was there. My mind went completely blank. I remarked to the driver, 'I must be losing my mind. I can't remember why I wanted to see Alan. Come on. Let's go.'

"We got back in the pick-up and continued down the highway. All of this took three or four minutes. We rounded a curve and there was my neighbor and his wife who had been driving right behind us, crushed to death by a coal truck. You described the scene of the accident exactly the way it happened."

I cannot explain why the Lord would allow an elderly couple to die in an accident that was meant for my brother. God is sovereign and only He can answer that question. But somebody was scheduled to die on the road that day. Morgan was not killed because somebody was standing in the gap and interceding for God to spare his life. Could it be that perhaps the elderly couple had nobody praying for them?

This incident brings to mind the story in Exodus where the Hebrew children put blood on their doorpost and, because of their covenant with God, the death angel passed over them. Those households that were not in blood covenant with God suffered the death of their firstborn. Later, when God wanted to destroy this same group of Hebrew people for their idolatry, Moses interceded for them and God spared their lives. Prayers of intercession still work today.

After this happened, Morgan woke up spiritually. His life began to change after that. He realized that he faced death and would have been instantly killed had it not been for the mercy of Almighty God.

Earlier in the book, I mentioned that Morgan stopped attending church over a conflict with a young man who brought a gun to church. I prayed earnestly for Morgan for many years. My prayer was, "Lord, you can't let Morgan die lost. He is the person who was responsible for leading me to the Lord. I don't want to see the person who led me to you die lost."

Morgan doesn't drink, but one day he stopped in a bar for a soft drink. In this same bar was the man who had caused the incident in the church decades earlier. Morgan had not seen him since that night in the church, but he still harbored so much bitterness and resentment that he was thinking to himself, "There's so and so. We're not in church now, so I hope he tries something with me. I'll stomp him in the floor."

Instead, the man saw Morgan and came toward him with his hand out. He said, "Morgan, is that you? Oh, Morgan, I've lived in hell for years. I can't believe what I did to you years ago in that church. I want you to know how sorry I am for what I did. I've often wondered if you're still alive. I've always wanted to tell you how sorry I am."

Morgan related that incident to me, and I said, "Morgan, you got your feelings hurt and lived with offense for decades. You allowed that one incident to destroy your relationship with the Lord. And now you find out that God has been dealing with this man about his own actions for years."

I had a dream that Morgan was traveling on a long journey and had only a very small suitcase to take along with him. I knew, and Morgan agreed, that the dream meant that when Morgan died, he would have very little to show for the work he had done on earth for the Lord. He allowed the enemy to waste all of the good years that he could have spent doing something worthwhile for the kingdom of God.

We cannot allow offense to affect our relationship with the Lord or with other people. Proverbs 18:19 tells us that a brother offended is harder to win than a strong city, and contentions are like the bars of a castle. When people are offended, the enemy will torment and defeat them. Offense causes us to become resentful and bitter, and it can cause us to lose our relationship with the Lord. We must live in forgiveness against those who have offended us, and if we have offended others, we must seek their forgiveness as well.

Be Sensitive to the Holy Spirit

It is important to listen to the voice of God and be sensitive and obedient to the Holy Spirit every day of your life. He knows of danger ahead of time. He knows who, what, when, where, and how. And just as He did with my brother Morgan, the Holy Spirit will even warn believers about danger that is facing unbelievers and those who have backslidden from God.

Being sensitive to the Holy Spirit requires obedience. For example, in the situation with Morgan, I had a strong impression to take my Bible and go to a quiet place where I could read. I obeyed. While I was in the Lord's presence, He gave me a vision and showed me everything that was planned. Then I went to a place where I could pray without interruption. I interceded for Morgan until I felt a breakthrough. You must keep your mind on God throughout the day in order for Him to use you in this manner.

Another reason that we need to keep our mind on God every day is because we are living in a time when any job is potentially dangerous. Look at the people who have been shot by a disgruntled employer, or the teachers who have been shot by students who brought a gun to school. Think of the people who died on September 11, 2001. Who would have thought that an office job in the Pentagon or the Twin Towers could have resulted in a fiery death that day? Yet, some people were warned by the Holy Spirit not to go to work that day. In other cases, unexplained events happened to make them late enough for work to miss the tragedy. Were their lives spared because somebody was interceding for them at the prompting of the Holy Spirit?

My late father-in-law, John Bava, was a young Spirit-filled believer when he had a warning experience while working in the coal mines. He was underground with his father, who also worked in the mines. John was digging the low seam of coal and his dad was digging the high seam.

As they were working, the Holy Spirit prompted John to look up at the high seam of coal. When he did, he saw it move. The Holy Spirit forcefully commanded him, "Step back! Step back!" He told his dad to step back, and both did so. Then a huge block of coal that weighed about two tons fell where they had been standing. Both would have been crushed to death if John had not obeyed the warning of the Holy Spirit.

An interesting side note to this story is that John's father, Pete, was not a believer at that time. Pete was an Italian immigrant who had been raised as a Roman Catholic, but he was not serving the Lord. He was often angry that his sons attended a "Holy Roller" church, and he did everything he could to keep them away from church.

But one day he became seriously ill and was close to death. Even though he made fun of Pentecostals, it was his sons and a Pentecostal minister who prayed a prayer of faith as Pete lay on his deathbed. The Lord healed him instantly, and Pete jumped out of bed and praised the Lord. He accepted Christ and was filled with the baptism of the Holy Spirit. He became a great witness for the Lord, and he never missed an opportunity to speak or testify of God's goodness. For the rest of his life, as long as he was physically and mentally able, he never missed a church service. He would say the service was "no good" if people didn't shout and praise the Lord.

Protection Through Revelation to Other Believers

Sometimes the Lord might give you a warning, but He will use the revelation and prayers of other believers to intercede on your behalf. Every believer should be sensitive and obedient to the Holy Spirit because we in the body of Christ need to depend on each other for prayers of faith and intercession.

One night I awoke about three a.m. and the Holy Spirit spoke to me. Three times I heard the words, "A truck driver." Thinking that perhaps something was happening outside, I got up and looked out the window. There was no truck outside, but those words remained in my mind.

Later I was driving to a revival, and this was still on my mind as I traveled. I preached from Sunday through Wednesday. In the Wednesday night service, two young ministers who were present came to me after church and said, "The Lord spoke before the service ended and said to lay hands on you and pray for your trip back to Cleveland." Several of the men prayed for me that night and asked the Lord to protect me while I traveled.

I said my farewells and left the church in Nashville, Tennessee to drive back home. As I neared the intersection of I-24 and I-75 around Chattanooga, I was driving between fifty-five and sixty miles per hour. I was not aware that I was falling asleep until I suddenly heard the horn of a tractor trailer. I became alert just as my car was ready to go underneath the rig of this tractor trailer. When the driver saw in his rearview mirror what was happening, he blew his horn and swerved to the right. I swerved to the left.

By giving me the warning, "a truck driver," the Lord was simply telling me to pray about a truck driver. At that time, I didn't know where or what was going to happen that involved a truck driver. The Holy Spirit impressed these men at the church to pray for my protection before I left that night. It was obviously an angel of the Lord that prompted the truck driver to glance in his rearview mirror just in time to take action. There is no question that those prayers saved my life that night, and they kept the trucker from being involved in an accident as well.

Another situation occurred years ago when, through a dream, the Lord told one of my church members that I would be called to see someone in a pickup truck. This man in the truck would rob me and attack me with a hunting knife. He even saw the color of the knife handle.

During a revival service one night, we received a phone call at the church. The phone was answered by our clerk, and she came to me with this message: A man is on the phone. He says he is at a bus station and needs money to get home. He wants to know if somebody can come there and help him.

I spoke to the man on the phone and told him that I would come to help him. Glendon Berg—the church member who had been given the dream—saw me leave and asked where I was going. I told him about the call and said, "I hate not to help him."

Glendon replied, "You're not going without me."

So he and I left and drove to the bus station. When we arrived, we noticed this man's truck sitting on the outskirts of the bus station. The man stepped out of his truck, and Glendon immediately got the feeling that this was his dream. We got out of the car, and Glendon stepped onto the man's running board. There on the seat was the very hunting knife the Lord had shown him in the dream

Immediately Glendon closed the truck door and stood between the door and this man who wanted money. We gave the man several dollars, and Glendon asked, "Do you deer hunt?"

"No, why do you ask?" the man replied.

"I see that you have a deer knife in your car," Glendon replied.

The man became flustered and could not give a reply.

Thankfully, the Lord used a godly and obedient church member to keep me out of trouble that night. In the body of Christ, we need each other!

Use Your God-Given Power and Authority

The Lord knows every problem and every trap the enemy has set for you, your family, your church, and the nations. If you pray often—especially in your prayer language of the Holy Spirit—and if you study the Bible and remain obedient and close to the Lord, the Holy Spirit will give you revelation to prepare you for future events. Often He does this so that you can use the power and authority He has given you to stop a plan of the enemy.

Why not use the power and authority of the Holy Spirit within you to stop the plans of the enemy? Touch the heart of God. Develop a close relationship with Him. Get the word of God in your heart and mind. When you do, the power of God through the Holy Spirit will show you things to come. Your prayerful intercession will have a mighty impact on your own life and the lives of those around you.

It is so important to listen to and obey the leading of the Holy Spirit. But your response to His warning is up to you. If you choose to ignore the warning, you or those you love will walk into snares and spiritual or physical death traps. You cannot ignore His warning and expect trouble not to follow. We should thank God for the gift of the Holy Spirit that warns us of those things ahead of time.

These are Perilous Times

We have seen terrible natural disasters hit the earth in our lifetime, yet there are more disasters to come. We have fought tragic wars throughout history, yet there are more wars to come. No longer do we turn on the news to hear about terrorism in some distant country. Today we have terrorists operating right here on our own soil.

I have seen in the spirit some of the things that are being planned by terrorists for this nation, and I'm telling you that these terrorists will stop at nothing to destroy our country and the rest of the world. The Holy Spirit has revealed coming attacks to me and many other believers as well. Planned attacks have been thwarted, and I believe it is the prayers of the saints of God that have cause these attacks to be exposed before they could be carried out.

Over a year ago, I was in prayer when the Holy Spirit revealed that great darkness would come out of Lebanon. In the Spirit, He allowed me to see fires throughout the country. As I write this, Israel and Lebanon have just ended a war, and I have seen this revelation from the Holy Spirit come to pass. The Holy Spirit has also shown me that a famine is coming to the Middle East.

We Must Pray, Fast, and Repent

The Bible tells us that, in the last days, evil will become worse and worse. In the gospels, when the disciples asked Jesus for the signs of His return and the end of the age, the reply that Jesus gave wasn't pleasant. He said there would be wars, rumors of wars, famines, pestilences, and earthquakes. The prophets of the Bible also saw terrible events coming upon the earth in the last days.

Through revelations of the Holy Spirit, the Lord has shown His people the plagues, bombings, earthquakes, tsunamis, and other terrible events that will continue to come upon our nation and the world. We are living in the last days, and we have been warned in scripture to expect these things.

I believe that some of these events can be stopped if we will pray, fast, and repent for the sins of our nation. But we must understand one thing: The cup of iniquity is nearly full. We cannot simply pray and fast; we must also have true repentance. We must turn from unrighteousness. Without prayer, fasting, and repentance for the sins of our nation, we cannot blame God, the devil, the President, or global warming for the problems that are going to come on the earth. We can only blame the sins of the nations.

Second Chronicles 7:13-14 says, *"When I shut up the heaven and there is no rain, or command the locusts to devour the land, or send pestilence among My people, if My people who are called by My name will humble themselves, and pray and seek My face, and turn from their wicked ways, then I will hear from heaven, and will forgive their sin and heal their land."*

People who claim to be Christians have a responsibility to repent and turn from their wicked ways. They have a responsibility to pray and seek God's mercy when the sins of a nation have brought judgment and plague. Notice in those two verses of scripture that God did not tell the prophets to strike the water with a staff so that healing would come to the land. He did not say that prayer alone would heal the land. He said that we must humble ourselves, pray, seek His face, and turn from sin and wickedness.

When Christians are living righteously before God, they will lead sinners to Christ. A backslider who is living an ungodly life cannot lead a sinner to the Lord. Jesus said that if the blind lead the blind, both will fall into a ditch.

People are not prepared for what is coming upon the earth. The Bible tells us that men's hearts will fail them for fear. Often, a person who brings that kind of message is accused of being pessimistic. Indeed, we find many Christians today who do not want to hear a message of sin, judgment, and repentance. They want to hear a positive message or no message at all.

But we are living in the last days, and the Bible clearly tells us that in the last days, judgment will come upon the earth. Still, God does not send judgment without first warning His servants who will listen. Are you listening? Who will a distraught nation of sinners and lukewarm Christians look to when judgment comes? Will they seek out the ministers and prophets who have brought forth a message of endless prosperity and earthly blessings? Or will they search out that those who are on fire for God and can minister to them in their distress?

If you are righteous, Spirit-filled, and living close to the Lord, ask Him to give you revelations of trouble on the horizon. Repent, fast, and seek God in fervent prayer. Stand in the gap and become a bridge of intercession for the nation. Spiritual hedges of protection can be rebuilt. Perhaps many of these judgments can be stopped and terrorist plots exposed before they can attack.

And if trouble does come, the Lord is able to keep you far away from danger if you will listen and be obedient to His voice.

God Still Speaks

While in prayer about a year ago, the Lord gave me this message through the Holy Spirit: "I am searching for people who will fast and pray and seek my face. I desire to give them revelations. I desire to tell them what the terrorists are planning. I desire to show them the future. I am looking for people who will be my spokesmen. I want to warn them, but where are those who will listen and be warned?"

It is heartbreaking to hear the Lord say that He is searching for people to whom He can speak and give revelation, but He cannot find many who will listen. God is looking for people who are willing to move away from the cares of this life, seek His face, and listen to His voice. He is looking for those who will tap into the very presence of God. Those who are listening to the Lord will see and hear everything that is going to happen before it happens.

Every believer needs to pray and seek the face of God for this nation and its leaders, as well as other nations and their leaders. We need to pray that the Lord will reveal Himself to them, that He will give all of them the wisdom of God, and that He will put people in positions of power who will listen to His servants when they have a prophetic word from the Lord.

In First John 4:4, we read that He who is in you—the Holy Spirit—is greater than he who is in the world. The Holy Spirit is your Helper, Comforter, Friend, Ally, Advocate, Advisor, and Strengthener. He convicts you of sin. He brings you into the presence of God. He motivates you to live a holy and pure life. He teaches, inspires, and reveals God's secrets. He helps you to worship and pray. He gives you peace and joy. He leads and guides you every step of the way.

Why should you be a half-hearted Christian when you can be the man or woman of God that He called you to be? The time will surely come when you will face difficult circumstances, and you will need the Holy Spirit in your life. Before you face those circumstances, take the time to learn the teaching of God on this subject and pray for the infilling, the gifts, and the anointing of the Spirit of the Living God. Remain humble before the Lord, and always give Him the praise, honor, and glory. If you do this, you will be amazed at how the Holy Spirit will operate in your life.

The baptism of the Holy Spirit is not just a doctrine of Pentecostal and Charismatic denominations. Many of us do not understand what we really have when we say that we are filled with the Holy Spirit. Perhaps if more of us truly understood Who is dwelling in us, the rest of the world would want what we have. Hosea 4:6 tells us that we are destroyed for lack of knowledge. Our lack of knowledge, combined with our unbelief and disobedience, means that the Holy Spirit is not accomplishing through most of us what He came to earth to accomplish.

Every demonic spirit and principality in Satan's kingdom wants to do battle with God's people. You have within you the power and authority to withstand every trial, every temptation, every affliction, and every hour of darkness that is coming upon the earth. The Holy Spirit Who dwells with you and in you will sustain you through every situation. You don't have to be defeated; you can overcome.

I hope this book has inspired you to desire the Holy Spirit and His manifestations every day and in every situation of your life. Speaking from personal experience, it is my opinion that you should not even drive your car unless the Holy Spirit is operating in your life. And today, because we live in such perilous times, it is important that the children of God operate in the fullness of the gifts of the Holy Spirit. We need His revelation to show us things to come.

Stay Connected

Do not become discouraged and lose faith when you see these things happening around the world. God is bringing a great harvest of souls into His kingdom in every part of the earth. We see this in countries like Africa, South America, and even Iran. The Chinese are coming to Christ at such a tremendous rate that, if statistics are correct, there are more believers in China right now than in America. Just like the Bible says, when we see these events taking place, and when the gospel is preached around the world, we know that the end is near.

The Holy Spirit connects you to God. Keep that connection strong. You can win every battle through unconditional surrender and obedience to the Holy Spirit. I want to encourage you to build a relationship with God and allow His Holy Spirit to connect you to the power, presence, and fullness of our Almighty God.

SECTION THREE
We Need the Fire

"So I say to you, ask and it will be given to you;
seek and you will find; knock and it will be opened to you.
For everyone who asks receives, and he who seeks finds,
and to him who knocks it will be opened.
If a son asks for bread from any father among you,
will he give him a stone?
Or if he asks for a fish,
will he give him a serpent instead of a fish?
Or if he asks for an egg,
will he offer him a scorpion?
If you then, being evil, know how to give good gifts to your children,
how much more will your heavenly Father give the Holy Spirit
to those who ask Him!"

LUKE 11:9–13

CHAPTER 12

Questions and Answers

Aren't we all filled with the Holy Spirit when we accept Christ and become born again?

Each person who becomes born again in Jesus Christ receives the Holy Spirit in his or her life. It is the Holy Spirit that draws a sinner to Christ. Without the Holy Spirit moving to convict you of sin, you would have never repented and confessed Jesus as your Savior. The moment that you confess your sins and ask Jesus to come into your life, the Holy Spirit brings forth new life and you become a new creation.

In John 20:22, when Jesus breathed on His disciples and said, "Receive the Holy Spirit," He was breathing new life into them. Just as the word of God is manifested through Jesus, the breath of God is manifested through the Holy Spirit. But it didn't stop there. After His disciples received the breath of new life, Jesus told them to wait in Jerusalem for the Promise of the Father. On that day, the Holy Spirit was *poured out*. The prophet Joel said:

"And it shall come to pass afterward, that I will pour out my Spirit upon all flesh; your sons and your daughters shall prophesy, your old men

shall dream dreams, your young men shall see visions: And also upon My menservants and upon My maidservants I will pour out my Spirit in those days" (Joel 2:28-29).

Peter quoted these verses and others from the book of Joel when he preached on the Day of Pentecost, after the outpouring in the upper room. His sermon is recorded in Acts 2:14-39.

When it comes to the Holy Spirit, we have a choice: We can either receive just enough of the Holy Spirit to become a new creature in Christ, or we can stand in the rain and collect buckets full of the Holy Spirit as it is poured out upon us. We can either get drenched in the Spirit of God, or we can stand underneath a big umbrella and stay dry while God rains down the Holy Spirit and His gifts to people all around us.

Does every person who receives the baptism of the Holy Spirit "speak with other tongues?"

While some believers place emphasis on the operation of the gifts of the Spirit as the initial evidence of the baptism of the Holy Spirit, most Pentecostals teach that the initial evidence of the baptism of the Holy Spirit is speaking with other tongues. This is how it happened on the Day of Pentecost: *"And they were all filled with the Holy Spirit and began to speak with other tongues, as the Spirit gave them utterance"* (Acts 2:4).

Sometimes people will pray to receive the baptism of the Holy Spirit, and the presence and power of God will be all over them. Yet they do not speak in tongues. Later, when they finally do speak in tongues, they say something like, "Oh, is *that* what that was? I started to pray those words several times but I didn't know what it was, so I didn't do it." They simply did not have enough knowledge of the baptism of the Holy Spirit to know that the Spirit was trying to pray through them.

There might be people reading this who have actually received the baptism of the Holy Spirit but have not spoken in tongues for this very reason. If you have prayed to receive the baptism and have felt the presence of God when you prayed, here is what I suggest. Pray and ask God to let you speak in your prayer language. Then start praising Him and speaking the words that He gives you to speak, even if they sound strange to you. There is a good chance that you will immediately start speaking in your heavenly prayer language.

When you are praying to receive the baptism of the Holy Spirit, you must open your mouth and speak to the Lord. Sometimes people come to the altar to receive the baptism, but they never open their mouth to pray. The Holy Spirit cannot pray through you if you don't open your mouth. Simply pray the prayer to be filled with the Holy Spirit; then start praising Him. Say "Thank you, Jesus," or "Hallelujah," or something along those lines.

Remember: a prayer language is for your personal edification and your spiritual strengthening. It allows close fellowship with the Lord. It gives you the ability to speak to God supernaturally. The Spirit prays when you don't know how to pray. Even though you may not understand what you are praying, you can be certain that you are speaking to God in a language that He understands. *"For he who speaks in a tongue does not speak to men but to God, for no one understands him; however, in the spirit he speaks mysteries"* (1 Corinthians 14:2).

Imagine how God must love His children to give us the ability to do this! Even the most unlearned and uneducated believer can speak things to God that the most educated man cannot comprehend. The sacredness of this gift is beyond human understanding.

Doesn't the Bible teach that tongues have ceased?

The Bible teaches that one day tongues *will* cease. There are people who teach that tongues *have* ceased, even though that is not what the Bible says. Here is their reasoning for that doctrine. In First Corinthians chapter 13, the apostle Paul talks about love being the greatest gift. He tells us that, even though we might operate in the gifts of tongues, prophecy, knowledge, and faith, if we don't have love, we are nothing. Love never fails. (There is no question that love should be the defining characteristic of all God's people, whether they are baptized in the Holy Spirit or not.)

Paul said that prophecies, tongues, and knowledge will someday vanish; but love will never vanish. We will know in part and prophesy in part until that which is perfect has come.

Those who believe tongues have ceased teach that the meaning of the phrase, "until that which is perfect has come," refers to the completion of the canon of Scripture in the first century. Therefore, they believe that prophecies, tongues, and knowledge vanished at the end of the first century.

But the rest of us teach that the meaning of the phrase, "until that which is perfect has come" refers to the completion of God's will and purposes on earth at the return of Jesus Christ. When Jesus returns to rule and reign, the knowledge of the Lord will cover the earth, the sea, and the skies. There will be no more need for the gifts of tongues, prophecy, or word of knowledge. But since God is love, we know—just like Paul said—that love will never vanish.

Throughout church history, people have spoken in tongues. The Azusa Street revival in 1906 began a new outpouring of the Holy Spirit and today, hundreds of millions of people around the world speak in tongues. They are living proof that tongues have not ceased.

It's embarrassing when someone speaks in tongues in church. Won't visitors think we're crazy?

At the outpouring on the Day of Pentecost, some of the crowd was amazed and perplexed, not understanding why all of these people suddenly started speaking in so many different languages. Others mocked and accused them all of being drunk.

In First Corinthians 14:20-25, Paul wrote about this very thing. He told the people that an unbeliever who comes to the church and hears people speaking in tongues might think they are out of their minds. The unbeliever simply does not understand what is happening.

But prophecy, which can come through the interpretation of tongues, is a supernatural sign to the unbeliever that God is in your midst. Paul writes that, through prophecy, the secrets of the unbeliever's heart are revealed, and he will fall on his face and worship God. That is one reason why tongues in a public setting must be interpreted. (The other reason is because tongues cannot edify those who are assembled unless there is an interpretation.)

I have seen the gift of interpretation of tongues used as a sign to the unbeliever. There is an example in this book of the Greek man who came to forcefully remove his wife from the church. An unbeliever might come into the church service and hear an interpretation of a message given in tongues. When the interpretation is supernaturally directed at the unbeliever, it convinces the person that God is truly present, because only God could have revealed the secrets that were spoken. Often, the unbeliever will come to Christ as a result of the spoken word.

If a person with no knowledge of tongues comes into a church service where the Holy Spirit is operating, that individual might have a few questions. There are many people who are now baptized with the Holy Spirit who knew nothing about the gift at one time. Some of those people once thought we were crazy; but now they've joined the crowd!

In First Corinthians 14:26-40, Paul wrote that tongues and interpretation should be done in an orderly manner, and he gave written instructions. But we should never be embarrassed about a move of the Holy Spirit in our churches. On the contrary; we should *desire* it.

I have seen people fall down when they are prayed for. Sometimes they stay on the floor for a while and sometimes they get right back up. What is that all about? Is it real or phony?

Sometimes the Holy Spirit comes upon people in such a powerful way that they cannot stand up. When that happens, they will often fall to their knees or lie prostrate on the floor. Just as rejoicing, laughing, and praising God are demonstrations of the Holy Spirit, so is falling under the power of God. It is very real.

In the early 1900s, after the outpouring of the Holy Spirit at Azusa Street, circuit riding preachers held outdoor revivals. Groups of skeptical men used any method possible to break up these revivals. They thought that people who fell under the power of God were all phonies. In one case, the men decided to prove it by poking people with boards full of hammered nails. But when the men poked the people with nails, the power of God was so strong that it traveled from the person on the ground, through the nail, into the board, and straight into the men holding the board. Those men fell to the ground and could not get up until they repented. It took just one poke for these men to learn the truth about the power of the Holy Spirit.

I will add that you do not have to fall to the floor to receive something from God. Nor should you try to push people down when you are praying for them. People are smart enough to know when they are being pushed. In fact, if somebody is praying for you and the power of God is not pulling you to the floor, you are not obligated to do a "courtesy fall." If the power of God isn't doing it, then there is no need to drop to the floor. It's that simple.

You talked about the anointing. What is that?

In scripture, to anoint means to consecrate holy people or holy things by rubbing them with oil. The oil is symbolic of the Holy Spirit. A person who is anointed is consecrated by the Holy Spirit to perform a service for God. The anointing is manifested as the powerful Spirit and presence of God working through a believer. It is a presence that is undeniable to both a believer and an unbeliever.

Isaiah 10:27 tells us that the anointing will lift our burdens and break the yoke of bondage. First John 2:27 says that the anointing of the Holy

Spirit will help us know truth and discern heresy. And Hebrews 1:9 says we are anointed with the joy of gladness.

In Luke 4:18-19, Jesus quoted the prophet Isaiah when He said, *"The Spirit of the Lord is upon Me, because He has anointed Me to preach the gospel to the poor; He has sent me to heal the brokenhearted, to proclaim liberty to the captives, and recovery of sight to the blind, to set at liberty those who are oppressed; to proclaim the acceptable year of the LORD."*

Since Jesus ministered on earth as a man, even He had to be anointed by the Holy Spirit to teach and perform miracles. Through the Holy Spirit, we can have that same anointing. When you spend time each day in prayer, when you study the word of God and let it change your life, when you fast, and when you remain humble and obedient before the Lord, you will feel that anointing. It is this anointing that enables you to have a powerful ministry or become a strong prayer intercessor. The power of God's anointing in your life will convict people of their sins and bring miraculous answers to prayer.

As a Spirit-filled believer, when you pray for people while you are under that anointing, it will flow from you and into other people when you touch them and pray for them. When the woman was healed by touching the hem of Jesus' garment, He knew that power had left His body (Mark 5:30). Jesus told His disciples that they would receive that same power when the Holy Spirit came upon them (Acts 1:8).

I have seen people operate under such an anointing that those for whom they pray will fall under the power of God without the anointed person ever touching them. In Acts 5:15, people brought the sick into the streets so that Peter's shadow would fall on them. Apparently Peter was under such a Holy Spirit anointing that even his shadow brought healing. In Acts 19:12, Paul was so anointed that his handkerchiefs and aprons caused diseases and evil spirits to leave the bodies of those who touched them.

God sometimes gives people a specific anointing; for example, some are anointed to pray for children. Some have an anointing to pray specifically for cancer and tumors. God wants the anointing to be present in every congregation. You should not have to wait for a special service when someone with an anointed ministry comes to town; it should operate in your own life and church.

Prophecy and word of knowledge sound like psychic power to me. What's the difference?

Words of knowledge and prophetic revelations come directly from God. Psychic power, divination, or any attempt to foretell the future by occult methods is a demonic counterfeit performed by familiar spirits. Occultism includes, but is not limited to, astrology, witchcraft, palm reading, and psychics. The Bible strictly forbids involvement in any type of sorcery, witchcraft, and other methods of the occult. People should stay away from such things. Involvement in occult activity opens the door for demonic possession and oppression in your life.

Demonic spirits cannot know anything about the future until God Himself first reveals it through a method that only God can use, such as scripture, a prophetic word, or a word of knowledge. It is true that Satan has tried to hijack God's gifts and convince people that the future can only be revealed through demonic methods. Therefore, when God reveals something to His children through one of the gifts of the Holy Spirit, even some who call themselves Christians believe that it must be of demonic origin.

It is God Almighty, the Creator of the universe, who holds the copyright on all gifts, including the word of knowledge and prophecy. Satan has tried to pervert and cheaply imitate everything that God created. There is no question that the enemy has tried to take God's spiritual gifts captive, but God is also in the business of setting captives free. Satan did not create the supernatural. The Almighty God did. And we, as believers in Christ, must take back what the devil has stolen.

If Satan has the ability to counterfeit these gifts, then how can I tell what is real and what is counterfeit?

When you hear or see something strange that does not line up with the Word of God, even if it comes from a Christian, you should question the manifestation. It might indeed a spirit, but it might not be the Spirit of God. The Bible tells us to examine and prove all things that claim to be of the Spirit of God. We should judge its content, its relevancy, and its alignment with God's word.

Here are some pertinent scriptures:

"Do not quench the Spirit. Do not despise prophecies. Test all things; hold fast what is good." (1 Thessalonians 5:19-21)

"Let two or three prophets speak, and let the others judge." (1 Corinthians 14:29)

"Beloved, do not believe every spirit, but test the spirits, whether they are of God; because many false prophets have gone out into the world. But by this you know the Spirit of God: Every spirit that confesses that Jesus Christ has come in the flesh is of God, and every spirit that does not confess that Jesus Christ has come in the flesh is not of God..." (1 John 4:1-3)

There are principles that can help you determine what is genuinely from the Holy Spirit and what is counterfeit:

- If the manifestation is genuinely from the Holy Spirit, it will magnify and glorify our Heavenly Father. If it glorifies anybody or anything else, it is not of God.

- It will edify, exhort, strengthen, encourage, and comfort the body of Christ.

- It must conform to the written Word of God. If the manifestation is contrary to scripture, it is not of God. To discern this, you must first have a good knowledge of the Bible. If you do not study His written Word, you become susceptible to any false doctrine or spiritual manifestation that is not from God.

- It must promote righteous living. If it encourages people to sin and live contrary to the Word of God, it is definitely not from God.

- If it promotes bondage or traditions of man, it is not from God.

- The person who is being used in the gift must be a sincere, Spirit-filled believer of good character who is living a holy life before

God. If the person is living a sinful life, he or she is likely operating through demonic powers.

- Does the prophecy come to pass? A true prophet of God does not "miss it." When someone speaks prophetically, how do we know what to believe if their prophetic word is not correct all the time? In my personal experience, the Lord is also very clear when He speaks prophetically. You will not have to manipulate the prophecy to make it appear that it came to pass.

Some people will be deceived by those who demonstrate counterfeit gifts. Even a person who appears to operate under an anointing can be a counterfeit; however, the Lord may allow it to continue for a while because He still wants those to whom they are ministering to receive a blessing. But there will come a time when God's mercy will end and He will deal strongly with the person who is operating under counterfeit gifts and anointing.

There will always be a few counterfeits among us, and the spirit of discernment will help you spot a phony. But don't let the fact that phonies exist discourage you from believing in God's gifts. Just because Satan is a counterfeiter does not mean that you throw out the legitimate things of God with the counterfeits of Satan. Do you stop using money just because a few people have the ability to successfully counterfeit bills? Of course not. Those who collect money are simply trained to discern the difference between a counterfeit and the real thing.

How do I judge the manifestations of the Holy Spirit?

We should always judge the manifestations of the Holy Spirit by the Word of God and by the results. Does the manifestation bring glory to God? Does it produce righteousness, joy, peace, and a greater love for the Lord? Does it bring sinners to repentance?

Matthew 7:15-20 tells us to beware of false prophets who come dressed in sheep's clothing, but inwardly they are ravenous wolves. We can know both true and false prophets by the fruits they bear. We should pay attention to things like character issues, selfishness and greediness, teaching that does not line up with scripture, and influence.

Critics will always be among us, so be careful that you don't judge Holy Spirit manifestations by the personal opinions of others. Those who argue against the work of the Holy Spirit are spiritually dry or dead. If you want to know if the manifestations of the Holy Spirit are real, ask those who have experienced them. Don't ask the scoffer who is full of unbelief.

I will admit that strange things happened years ago, when the Charismatic movement was still in its birthing years. For example, there were some who tried to teach people to speak in tongues. But you cannot teach someone to speak in tongues; a prayer language must come from God and only God. Some tried to teach people to prophesy by having them practice on each other, while giving them instruction that it was okay if they "missed it." There were others who thought that most of their church members were demon possessed. They couldn't hold a church service without trying to cast demons out of half the congregation.

These folks might have meant well, but their actions were not biblically based. Again, you need knowledge of the Bible and spiritual discernment, because the Holy Spirit will reveal to you what is real and what is not. The Lord does not mind when you humbly come before Him to ask if something is real.

Sincerely questioning a manifestation is one thing, but do not get into mockery of the Holy Spirit. This opens the door to oppression and possession by evil spirits. God will sometimes allow judgment to come upon people who mock and criticize the power of the Holy Spirit.

Years ago, my father-in-law John Bava attended a revival and went to the altar one night to pray with an individual who had been seeking the baptism of the Holy Spirit. While they were praying, the evangelist told them to get out of the church because that baptism of the Holy Spirit was not of God. He told them that they were not going to pray for it in that church.

John said, "We don't want stay in this church if the Holy Spirit is not welcome." He immediately got up from the altar, and he and Lucy left the church. Later that week, they learned that every person in the church got up and left after the evangelist made that statement. Two weeks later, the evangelist died.

John also told the story of hearing a minister on the radio who was making fun of people speaking in tongues. Suddenly the man started coughing and almost choked to death right there on the radio.

Even if you do not believe in the baptism or the manifestations of the Holy Spirit, I would strongly advise that you not be critical or make fun of those who do.

You said the Holy Spirit would warn us of things to come. A family member of mine died in a terrible accident. Why didn't the Lord warn me of this before it happened?

That is a question that only the Lord can answer. I can give my perspective based only on personal experience and knowledge of the Word of God.

If you are a Spirit-filled believer who prays daily and is sensitive and obedient to the voice of God, then I believe He would have warned you if prayer could have changed the situation. If He did not warn you, then perhaps the accident was simply going to happen, and there was nothing you could have done to stop it.

There is, without question, a covenant of protection for the children of God. We see this in Exodus 12:7 when the Hebrew children placed the blood of a lamb on their doorpost so that the death angel would pass them by. That was a picture of the protective power of the blood of Jesus, who would become the sacrificial Lamb.

The Bible is full of scriptures that tell us the Lord will protect us. Read Psalm 91, for example. It tells us that God is our refuge and our fortress. He will deliver us from the snare of the fowler, from perilous pestilence, from terror by night, from the arrow that flies by day, and from destruction. No evil or plague will come near us. He will give His angels charge over us.

That is powerful protection! No police officer or military presence can offer you that kind of assurance. I believe that as children of the Most High God, we can pray that protection over ourselves and our families.

There is also no doubt in my mind that the Holy Spirit of God, who knows all future events, will warn us of things in advance if they can be stopped. Our response to the warning is up to us. We can either ignore it and do what the Holy Spirit warned us not to do, or take action according to the word that we received. For example, if you are driving to the grocery store and the Holy Sprit burdens you to pray at that very moment, you cannot continue to the store and shop. You must pull over to the side of the road, have somebody else drive, or go someplace where you can pray. The enemy has something planned at that moment, and you must intercede immediately.

Could the person who was involved in the tragic event have received, but ignored, a prompting of the Holy Spirit? An example of this is our automobile accident in the 1960s. The Holy Spirit tried to delay me, then warned me two times to take another route. By not listening, we could have all been killed.

What about collective warnings? For example, let's assume that people are warned to evacuate their city because of a coming hurricane. If people choose to ignore the warning, the only people who can be blamed if there are deaths are those who ignored the warning.

The bottom line is this. The Lord is sovereign, and only He knows for certain why tragic events happen to you and to those you love. We know from scripture that man born of woman is of few days and full of trouble (Job 14:1). We know that the sun rises on the evil and the good, and it rains on the just and the unjust (Matthew 5:45). I want to encourage you, regardless of the circumstances, not to live with guilt and not to become angry at God. He has reasons that you will not understand until you get to heaven.

Life on earth is but a vapor compared to eternity. What if the death of that individual caused just one sinner to come to Christ? If your loved one was a believer in Christ, then in the mind of God, their death was worth it all. And we should not fret when we know that we will be with them again for eternity.

How can I learn to listen to the Holy Spirit?

Some people do not believe that God speaks to us today. But Jesus said in John chapter ten that His sheep know His voice and follow Him. Every believer can learn to listen to the voice of the Lord. When we talk about hearing the voice of the Lord or the voice of the Holy Spirit, here are some guidelines that I use in my own life:

- First, you will not likely hear an audible voice, although it can and does happen. Instead, the Holy Spirit will speak to your spirit in one of several ways. Perhaps you will have a nudge or an inner leading. A thought might drop quickly into your spirit. He could speak while you are praying or reading the Bible, and you will get an undeniable quickening of the Holy Spirit. Regardless of the method He uses, it will not leave your mind. You simply cannot get away from it.

- Sometimes you will feel a strong impression toward someone. Weigh it out and pray about it. If it stays in your spirit, it is likely from the Lord. Just make sure the leading is controlled by the Holy Spirit and not by your own flesh.

- You will sense an inward peace from God when you are doing the right thing. Pay attention to restlessness in your spirit. Sometimes people brush off their restlessness and explain it away with excuses that might seem logical. But if you do not have peace about something and are feeling restless, you need to reevaluate, pray, and seek the face of God to know His perfect will in that situation. You can always ask the Lord to stop whatever you are getting ready to do if it is not His will.

■ Learn when God is giving you a prayer burden. A burden is a weight or pressure that God places on you, giving you a feeling that you must get away from everything and get alone with God to pray. Obey and God will speak to you. When God gives you a prayer burden, it will be easier for you to pray for longer periods of time.

■ Sometimes the Holy Spirit will try to get you to a place where you can be quiet. You will feel a strong leading to get alone with the Lord because He wants to talk to you. Do not fight this; immediately obey the Lord.

■ When a person's face comes before you, when someone comes to your mind, or when you have a strong burden to pray for someone, do it immediately. Do not wait. If you do not know how to pray for the person, pray in the Spirit, because the Spirit knows how to pray in every situation. Pray until you feel a release.

■ Anytime you are warned about something—for example, through a vision, a dream, or a prophetic word—take that as a sign to pray. Intercede for that person or situation immediately because your intercession might stop what is being planned. Believers can intercede because they have a covenant with God. Abraham interceded for

Sodom and Gomorrah, and God protected Lot. Your children might be living in disobedience, but because you have a blood covenant with God, they can be protected through your prayers. Intercession simply means standing in the gap and becoming a bridge between that person and God. He will move on that person's behalf because of your prayers.

■ Write down dreams and visions and ask the Lord to give you the interpretation. People dream constantly; but if the dream is a spiritual one, you will remember it in great detail after you wake. You will sense that it is a spiritual dream, even when you do not understand the meaning right away.

■ The Holy Spirit will not speak nonsense to a person, nor will He bring confusion. He will speak something that will help you, and He will speak with a spiritual purpose in mind.

The apostle Paul warned that there are many voices in the world. We must be able, through prayer, fasting, and Bible study, to discern the many voices. There are spiritual voices, demonic voices, and carnal voices of our flesh. This is why we must learn to identify and listen to the voice of the Lord and ask for the gift of spiritual discernment.

If you listen to the Holy Spirit, you will avoid many problems for yourself, your family, and your church. If you don't listen, you will find yourself dealing with the same problems over and over. Learn to listen and obey so that you won't have to learn all of your lessons the hard way.

My church doesn't teach baptism and gifts of the Spirit. If this is real, then why do some pastors not teach these things?

Perhaps the number one reason some pastors do not teach these things is because their church denominational doctrine teaches against the infilling and gifts of the Holy Spirit. Some churches even teach that these manifestations are demonic. Others say the gifts died with the last apostle. If those things were all true, wouldn't drunken men in bars be laying hands on people and seeing them healed? And how could hundreds of millions of Christians around the world have received gifts that died with John the apostle?

By specifically teaching against this, or by forbidding their church members to engage in these practices, denominational leaders are overstepping their bounds of authority and placing themselves above God. They are claiming to know better than God what is best for their congregation. Recently, one major denomination said they would forbid their missionaries to use a private prayer language on the mission field. Yet, if anybody needs a prayer language and the gifts of the Holy Spirit, it is missionaries who are risking their lives to serve in areas of the world that are hostile to Christianity!

We are living in a time when it should be impossible for a minister *not* to believe in the baptism and gifts of the Holy Spirit. The evidence is everywhere. Hundreds of millions of people throughout the world today are baptized in the Holy Spirit. There are eighty-five million Spirit-filled believers on the continent of Africa alone.

Near Chattanooga, Tennessee is a large Baptist church called Abbas House. The pastor of this church, Ron Phillips, received the baptism of the Holy Spirit with the evidence of speaking in tongues, and he lost quite a few church members because of it. But since then, his church has experienced astonishing growth, and they have gained many more members than they lost. There is so much anointing of God present in his church that it puts many Pentecostal churches to shame.

This can happen in your church, too. God is pouring out His Spirit throughout the earth, and He doesn't want to leave your church in the dry, parched desert. If we believe the Word of God when it says that God is the same yesterday, today, and forever, then we have to believe that God did not become incapacitated after John died.

We all have a perspective of the Holy Spirit based on our religious background. And it is those preconceived ideas that cause people to question the move of the Holy Spirit. People who criticize the work of the Holy Spirit don't seem to understand that they are not criticizing us; they are criticizing God. Those folks will not have the joy of the Lord in their lives, and their ministry and prayer life will be very dry. Isn't it too bad that these ministers don't know what they're missing?

Why do we not see more of the power of God in our lives and churches today?

The short answer is that the Holy Spirit abides only in the hearts of those who welcome Him. The long answer is that there are several reasons why we do not see more of the power of God in our lives and churches today. Here are several of them:

Unbelief. I'll use this incident as an example. America witnessed a great healing revival in the 1940s and 1950s, and Oral Roberts was one of the men whom God used greatly in the gift of divine healing. But a jealous minister from Roberts' own denomination wrote a book outlining the reasons why, in this man's opinion, Oral Roberts was a fraud. Do you think God is going to move in an environment of unbelief like that?

In Matthew 13:54-58, we read that even Jesus could not do many mighty works when unbelief was present. Unbelief is sin. When we have unbelief, we don't really believe that God can or will do what He says He will do. We fail to believe that God is the same yesterday, today, and forever.

Lukewarm churches. There are too many dead or lukewarm churches, like those in Sardis and Laodicea that John wrote about in the third chapter of Revelation. They are neither hot nor cold. They are rich and have need of nothing. They have a form of godliness, but no power. They are full of spiritually lazy and weak Christians. According to John, a lukewarm church is nauseating to God. Why would God manifest His power to a church that nauseates Him? These people have a God-given ability to affect their family and the world around them. But they forfeit it through laziness, carnality, disobedience, pride, and unbelief.

Wrong emphasis. There are churches today that place more emphasis on the size of their church building, the comfort of their seating, and the quality of the church's amenities than they do on the spiritual condition of their church members. Leaders spend more time learning about the church growth movement than they do the movement of the Holy Spirit.

But when the Holy Spirit is moving mightily in a church and the gifts of the Spirit are operating, it won't matter where the church meets or what the building looks like. People will be drawn there to witness the power of God. Even sinners will come to see the action. Once people have experienced God's power and anointing, they will want to be wherever God is manifesting Himself through the gifts of the Holy Spirit.

Abandonment of truth. In John 14:16-17, Jesus called the Holy Spirit the Spirit of Truth. Some ministers, in their desire to be inoffensive, have abandoned Truth. The Holy Spirit will not abide in those who abandon Truth. He dwells only in those who worship the Lord in Spirit and in Truth. Do not expect a move of God if your church has abandoned the Truth.

Early in my ministry, the Lord told me, "Just preach the gospel and proclaim the good news. Tell the people what I did for them on Calvary." Today we find ministers who no longer want to preach the true gospel message: That Jesus came to earth, died on a cross, and redeemed us for eternity through His shed blood.

People need to be challenged to grow in the knowledge and the Spirit of the Lord. There is nothing wrong with a message of encouragement, and there is nothing wrong with teaching people how to live more productive lives. But why are we leaving out the message of salvation, the cross, the blood of Jesus, sanctification, and the baptism of the Holy Spirit? Why are we ashamed of the Gospel?

We think we're too smart. We have allowed intellectualism to become a substitute for a move of God. Education and sensitivity to the Holy

Spirit do not have to be at odds with each other, but often they are. The Bible tells us that we must study to show ourselves approved. But we cannot cram God into a theological box and expect Him to do great things in our midst. Pride and arrogance will cause people to think they know better than God Himself how to handle things. People tend to analyze based on knowledge and circumstances instead of listening to the direction of the Lord.

Lack of prayer, fasting, and Bible reading. Too many Christians have a lack of hunger to experience more of God. We cannot squeak out a five minute prayer and expect to enter the presence of God. And without fasting, some prayers are not going to be answered. We cannot have knowledge of the Word of God if we never crack open the Bible. Many thoughts and activities distract us each day, and sometimes it becomes difficult to pray and read the Bible. But scripture can be used to discipline yourself, to quiet your thoughts, and to think on the things of God.

A mighty move of God does not come by attending church for an hour on Sunday and rushing out by noon to beat the crowds at the restaurant. When your own selfish desires are more important than God, then you cannot expect Him to move greatly in your midst. Instead of watching television or surfing the Internet, try spending more time in the presence of God. Teach your children to do this as well. If we desire a move of the Holy Spirit in our midst, we cannot make God take a back seat to the cares of this life. We must put Him in the driver's seat.

Sin in the church. When the congregation—and even the pastor—are willfully sinning against God, the Holy Spirit will not move in that church. But when the pastor and most of the congregation are Spirit-filled, and when the gifts of the Spirit are operating in the church, the Holy Spirit will move in their midst. The Holy Spirit can even give a word of knowledge through the interpretation of tongues to expose sin in the congregation. God does this so that the sinner will heed God's word that was spoken through His servant and come to repentance.

As the shepherd of the flock, every pastor has a crucial responsibility to live a godly life, to preach the true word of God, and to lead the congregation along a path of righteousness. If a pastor stands in the pulpit to preach while living a life of unrepentant sin, that pastor has lost the fear of God. That is a dangerous place to be. Why risk experiencing the judgment of God for unrepentant sin and hypocrisy? Eventually the sin will be exposed, because God will not tolerate you calling yourself a Christian and holding an office in His church while engaging in sinful behavior. He will give you an opportunity to repent. If you do not repent, He will expose your sin to bring you back into covenant with Him and to clear the disgrace you have brought to His name.

We get in God's way. We need to get out of the way and let the Holy Spirit move the way God wants Him to move. We need to give up control and give up our preconceived ideas of how God operates. Let Him do His work on the earth today in whatever fashion He chooses. Then be obedient to what He tells you to do.

What can the church do to see more signs and wonders, and more of the operation of the gifts of the Spirit today?

In 1954, a minister recommended that I attend a holy convocation. While I was there, a man from Brooklyn, New York named B. E. Johnson walked up to me and, not knowing me or anything about me, gave me a prophetic word. He said, "The Lord says to you, 'Call upon me and I will show you great and mighty things. Fast, pray, and seek my face. Seek me. I will do mighty miracles through you when you seek me in fasting and prayer.' "

That is the key to signs and wonders. First, the church needs to pray. And when I say pray, I'm not talking about a five minute corporate prayer where you lift up the needs of the congregation on Sunday morning. I am talking about fervent, effectual prayer. I'm talking about prayer meetings and powerful intercession. Most churches today no longer have prayer meetings because, when they did, nobody showed up. Do not expect to see a move of God in any form if you and your church do not pray.

But bold Spirit-filled believers who fast and fervently pray can humbly call upon the Lord to confirm His word with signs, wonders, and miracles (Acts 14:3). He wants to do this to show the world that the message of the gospel is real. Preach with the anointing and the power of the Holy Spirit and expect manifestations. This will reach even the unbelievers.

Other nations are filled with people who have limited knowledge of God. Their religions have included voodoo, witchcraft, and worship of false gods and demonic spirits. These people are accustomed to experiencing activity in the demonic spirit realm. When a Christian tells them that God is more powerful than the spirits they serve, that minister must be able to back up his words with signs and wonders.

One thing that I noticed during my ministry was this: The hungrier the church was for supernatural manifestations of the Holy Spirit, the more the Holy Spirit operated in their midst. The church in Northern Virginia was hungrier for a supernatural move of God than any other church where I served as pastor. Many of the incidents that I tell in this book happened in that church. I believe the Lord saw and honored their desire for more of Him, and the supernatural move of the Holy Spirit helped that church to grow.

A Spirit-filled believer who hungers and thirsts for God's presence and who operates in the gifts of the Spirit will be a blessing to any church and community. That is a person who will have a strong desire to resist sin and temptation. People who seldom pray, who neglect to read God's word, who have little spiritual hunger, and who compromise with the world will not be used mightily by God. I have never seen it happen.

What practical tips can you offer to people who desire more of the Holy Spirit in their lives?

Here are some things that have worked in my own life:

- Pray every day. Prayer is a spiritual discipline, and you should never let anything or anybody hinder you from having regular devotional time with the Lord. Once you no longer pray regularly, you will have a difficult time establishing that regular devotional time. You cannot develop a relationship with God unless you are disciplined to pray.

- When you pray, go to a place where you will not be distracted. Turn off the television. Some people prefer to have soft worship music playing while they pray, and that is fine. But don't have noise that will distract you from prayer.

■ If I plan to spend an hour with the Lord, I will usually start by reading some scripture. Then I approach the Father reverently, and I begin to thank and praise Him for who He is, for sending Jesus to earth for our salvation, and for the blessing of the Holy Spirit. Philippians 4:6 tells us, *"Be anxious for nothing, but in everything with prayer and supplication, with thanksgiving, let your requests be made known to God."* Before you start asking Him for things, you are supposed to thank Him for who He is and for what He has already done.

■ Pray often in your prayer language of the Holy Spirit. When you don't know the words to pray, the Holy Spirit will pray for you.

■ When you sense a strong desire to pray, never brush it off. Pray immediately, and keep praying until you feel a release. That release, coupled with a sense of peace, means that the Lord has answered your prayer.

■ When you pray, it is not necessary for you to talk constantly. Sometimes you need to be quiet and let the Lord speak to your spirit. You do need to talk to Him, of course, but it should be a two-way conversation. Wait on the Lord and He will speak.

■ When He speaks, you need to be obedient. If you stop obeying, He will stop speaking and guiding you.

■ Before I go to sleep at night, I praise the Lord, thank Him for sending Jesus, thank Him for giving us revelations through the

Holy Spirit, and so forth. When I go to sleep, my spirit is already in contact with God. In times like that, the Lord will reveal things to me in dreams.

■ Churches should have regular prayer meetings. The body of Christ should be interceding regularly for lost souls, for our nation, and for the nations of the world. It was a regular prayer meeting that brought the spiritual awakening in the town where I grew up. Before every church service, there was a prayer meeting that lasted about an hour. At the altars, they prayed for at least another hour. Prayer works.

■ Don't forget to fast. Most people should have no problem fasting one day a week. Sometimes you will be led to fast for three days or longer. When I fast for up to three days, I do not eat any food at all. I just drink water. In my early revivals, I often ate only one meal a day during the entire one or two week revival. When you fast, the Spirit of God will come upon you, and He will give you revelations and answers to prayer. Like prayer, fasting is also a spiritual discipline.

■ You must read and study the Bible. You need knowledge. Before I was called to preach, I spent one, two, or three days at a time doing nothing but praying and reading the word of God. I had a goal to memorize the entire New Testament, but I didn't quite make it. It is very important to know what God says to us in His word. If you don't have that much time to read, get the Bible on CD and listen to it as you travel or as you work around the house.

- You need spiritual maturity to be used by God in the fullness of the gifts. God will test you and place you in the wilderness, and that is one of His methods of teaching you. This process takes time, and the only way you can hurry through the testing process is to learn your lessons the first time.

- Be sensitive to the Holy Spirit and allow him to move in your life the way He chooses.

- Whatever you want from the Lord—whether it be faith, the gift of discernment, or any other gift—ask Him for it. If He knows that you desire the gift and will use it humbly to magnify the Lord, He will give you what you desire.

- Fear God more than you fear man. When you fear man more than you fear God, you will lose whatever spiritual power and authority God might have given you. Remember that, in the end, you will stand before God—not man—and give an account for everything you have done in this life.

Why do you think some Christians do not seeks spiritual gifts?

Some people accept the teaching that the baptism and gifts of the Holy Spirit are no longer operational. Others think the gifts are optional and, therefore, they can live without them. Some believers have never been encouraged to seek spiritual gifts. If the gifts are not operational in their church, and if they never hear teaching on the topic, they might simply lack knowledge of the infilling and gifts of the Holy Spirit.

And some people, I regret to say, are just spiritually lazy. They know the gifts exist, but they don't care to receive them.

You can be saved without the gifts of the Spirit; but with them, you will mighter in God. We are living in a day when every believer needs these gifts, so I want to encourage everybody to get down to business with the Lord and do as Paul said—earnestly desire the gifts!

Do you think that Spirit-filled believers today fully understand the power of the Holy Spirit?

I don't think there are many people alive today who fully understand the enormous power of the Holy Spirit. Most of us don't come close to witnessing the power that the apostles saw in the early church.

Here is a great example. In Acts chapter eight, Phillip preached to a eunuch and then baptized him in water. When they came up from the water, the Spirit of the Lord caught Philip away, and the eunuch saw him no more. Then Philip showed up at Azotus. He passed through the city and preached all over the area until he came to Caesarea.

Did you catch that? The Holy Spirit carried Philip away to another city! This was not demonically inspired "soul travel" that some New Age adherents practice, where they consciously will their spirit and soul to leave their body. I want to emphasize that the Holy Spirit carried Philip's entire body, soul, and spirit to Azotus. How many times have you read that account in the Bible and skipped right over those verses without stopping to think about the miracle involved in that incident?

Here is another event that we often read without considering the miracle—not to mention the humor—involved in this incident. When

Balaam's donkey was stopped by an Angel of the Lord, it was evidently the Spirit of God who spoke through the donkey and made it talk to Balaam. The donkey said, "What have I done to cause you to hit me three times?" And oddly enough, Balaam replied, "You've mocked me! If I had a sword right now, I'd kill you!"

In the New Testament, Jesus walked on water and so did Peter. Once Peter received the baptism of the Holy Spirit, his very shadow brought healing to the sick. Jesus took Peter, James, and John onto a mountain, where He was transfigured before their eyes. Moses and Elijah also appeared.

If Christians experienced some of those things today, fear would send most to an early grave. And if you experienced those things and confessed to it, before long, somebody would be on the radio or an Internet site calling you a nut or a heretic. What a shame that so many Christians think of God as a weakling, yet consider the enemy so powerful.

The Holy Spirit gives us power and authority over the enemy. Think about the concept of authority. According to *Strong's Concordance,* the Greek word is exousia, and it means "ability or strength with which one is endued." It denotes the power of one whose commands must be obeyed. Who must obey our commands? Demon spirits that have been defeated by Jesus at the cross. Diseases. Human hurts. Luke 9:1-2 tells us that when Jesus sent out His disciples, He gave them power and authority over all demons. He gave them power and authority to cure diseases. He sent them to preach the kingdom of God and to heal the sick.

Is it possible, in our modern times, to see that same power of the Holy Spirit? Of course it is. God is the same yesterday, today, and forever. He has not changed; we have. He is not in a box; we are. The question is this: Do we want to spiritually commit our lives to Christ to the extent necessary to see that kind of powerful manifestation of the Holy Spirit?

If I receive the baptism of the Holy Spirit, can I lose the gift?

If you have backslidden away from God; if you find that you no longer pray in your prayer language; or if the gifts of the Spirit are no longer operating in your life, you need to repent of any sin in your life and pray for a renewed infilling of the Holy Spirit.

When you receive the baptism of the Holy Spirit, you need to maintain the gift by praying often, and praying in the Spirit. You also should engage in praise and worship on a regular basis. And of course, you must live a holy and sanctified life. You can keep the Holy Spirit in your life by maintaining a close and obedient relationship with Christ, and by praying often in your prayer language.

I will also add that just because someone can still speak in tongues does not mean that person is still living close to the Lord. There are definitely backslidden people—not many, but a few—who still try to speak in tongues. But with a little bit of discernment, the phonies will stand out like a flashing neon light. When my children were young, even they had no problem spotting them.

I did some terrible things in my life before I became a Christian. Can the Lord still use me in these gifts?

To answer that question, we need look no further than the Bible. Moses murdered a man before God called him to lead the Israelites out of

Egyptian bondage. King David was an adulterer and a murderer who was living with hidden sin until he repented after he was confronted by the prophet Nathan. Rahab was a prostitute who eventually became the great-great grandmother of King David. The apostle Paul was a murderer and a great persecutor of Christians before his conversion on the road to Damascus.

That same Paul, the ex-murderer, wrote in First Corinthians 6:9-11:

"Do you not know that the unrighteous will not inherit the kingdom of God? Do not be deceived. Neither fornicators, nor idolaters, nor adulterers, nor homosexuals, nor sodomites, nor thieves, nor covetous, nor drunkards, nor revilers, nor extortioners will inherit the kingdom of God. And such were some of you. But you were washed, but you were sanctified, but you were justified in the name of the Lord Jesus and by the Spirit of our God."

The Bible is clear. If you have repented of your sins, are living righteously and humbly before the Lord, He can certainly use you in the gifts.

If I have never received the baptism of the Holy Spirit, how do I receive this gift in my life?

The Holy Spirit is a free gift from God to His righteous and obedient children. If you have a hunger and thirst for the baptism of the Holy Spirit, He can be yours this day.

In Luke 11:9-13, we read where Jesus said, *"So I say to you, ask and it will be given to you; seek and you will find; knock and it will be opened to you. For everyone who asks receives, and he who seeks finds, and to him who* knocks it will be opened. If a son asks for bread from any father among you, will he give him a stone? Or if he asks for a fish, will he give him a serpent instead of a fish? Or if he asks for an egg, will he offer him a scorpion? If you then, being evil, know how to give good gifts to your children, how much more will your heavenly Father give the Holy Spirit to those who ask Him?"

If you have never accepted Jesus as your personal Saviour, you must first pray a prayer of repentance. The Bible tells us many things about sin and salvation:

"For all have sinned and fall short of the glory of God." (Romans 3:23)

"For God so loved the world that He gave His only begotten Son, that whoever believes in Him should not perish but have everlasting life. For God sent not His son into the world to condemn the world, but that the world through Him might be saved." (John 3:16-17)

"He who believes in Him is not condemned; but he who does not believe is condemned already, because he has not believed in the name of the only begotten Son of God." (John 3:18)

"If you confess with your mouth the Lord Jesus and believe in your heart that God has raised Him from the dead, you will be saved. For with the heart one believes unto righteousness, and with the mouth confession is made unto salvation." (Romans 10:9-10)

Perhaps you once asked Jesus into your heart but are no longer living close to the Him. You, too, should repent of your sins and rededicate your life to Him.

First, from your heart, pray a prayer of salvation and cleansing:

Heavenly Father, I thank you for loving me so much that you sent your Son, Jesus, to die on a cross for my sins. I accept His free gift of salvation, and I ask you to forgive me of my sins and give me eternal life. Cleanse me of all my unrighteousness. Remove bitterness, unforgiveness, anger, strife, pride, greed, rejection, and rebellion from my life. I forgive and release those who have harmed me and wronged me. Cleanse me of everything I have been involved in that is ungodly in your sight. Break the strongholds in my life. Break the power that I have given the enemy over my soul.

Help me to live righteously according to your word. I accept the victory and freedom that I now have in Christ Jesus. Help me to know your will for my life. Thank you for saving me and giving me your free gift of eternal life. I pray this in Jesus' name, Amen.

Once you have prayed a prayer of salvation and cleansing, the Lord can fill you with the baptism of the Holy Spirit. Here is a prayer to receive that gift:

Heavenly Father, I believe the Holy Spirit is real. I believe this gift is for me. Lord, I love you, and I want above all else to be filled with your Holy Spirit. I am asking you now to fill me with the baptism of the Holy Spirit. Give me the experience like the Christians had in the book of Acts. Fill me and use me with your gifts. I will humble myself and use this blessing only for your glory. In Jesus' name, Amen.

If you do not speak in tongues right away, keep praying, thanking

Him for the gift, and praising the Lord. You might receive your prayer language when you least expect it.

You should be baptized in water right away. Mark 16:16 says, "He who believes and is baptized will be saved." It is possible to receive the baptism of the Holy Spirit without first being baptized in water, but do not neglect this important step of water baptism.

Scripture for Personal or Group Study

What action did the Holy Spirit perform in these Old Testament references to the Spirit of God?

Genesis 41:25-41

Exodus 28:1-4

Exodus 31:1-11

Exodus 35:30-35

Numbers 11:25-30

Judges 3:7-11

Judges 11:29-33

Judges 13:18-25

Judges 14:5-6

Judges 14:19

Judges 15:11-17

1 Samuel 10:1-13

1 Samuel 16:1-13

2 Samuel 23:1-2

1 Kings 18:11-12

2 Kings 2:1-16

2 Chronicles 20:14-18

Psalm 51:10-13

Isaiah 11:1-2

Isaiah 48:16-17

Isaiah 59:19

Isaiah 61:1-3

Ezekiel 2:1-7

Ezekiel 3:10-15

Ezekiel 8:1-4

Ezekiel 36:24-27

Joel 2:28-29

Micah 3:8

Haggai 2:5

Zechariah 4:6

Why does a watchman over the nations have such an important job?

Ezekiel 33:1-11

What mighty acts did the Spirit of God perform in the life of Ezekiel?

Ezekiel 1:1-28   Ezekiel 11:1-24   Ezekiel 37:1-14

What mighty acts did the Holy Spirit perform in the life of the prophet Daniel?

Daniel chapter 2   Daniel chapters 4 – 6   Daniel chapters 9 – 12
Daniel chapter 3   Daniel chapters 7- 8

How was the Holy Spirit active within those connected to the birth of Jesus?

Matthew 1:18-21   Luke 1:5-16   Luke 1:57-80
Luke 1:26-38   Luke 1:39-45   Luke 1:25-35

What was the purpose of the Holy Spirit in these New Testament references?

Matthew 3:11   Matthew 10:16-20   Luke 4:16-22
Matthew 3:16   Mark 13:9-11
Matthew 4:1   Luke 4:13-15

How did the Holy Spirit empower Jesus and manifest in His ministry?

Matthew 3:13-17   Matthew 8:1-4   Matthew 8:16-17
Matthew 4:1-11   Matthew 8:5-13   Matthew 8:23-27
Matthew 4:23-25   Matthew 8:14-15   Matthew 8:28-34

Matthew 9:1-8	Mark 1:21-28	Luke 5:17-26
Matthew 9:18-26	Mark 2:1-12	Luke 6:17-19
Matthew 9:27-31	Mark 4:35-41	Luke 8:26-39
Matthew 9:32-34	Mark 5:35-43	Luke 8:40-48
Matthew 9:35-38	Mark 6:53-56	Luke 8:49-56
Matthew 14:13-21	Mark 7:24-30	Luke 9:37-42
Matthew 14:22-33	Mark 7:31-37	Luke 13:10-17
Matthew 14:34-36	Mark 8:1-9	John 2:1-11
Matthew 15:21-28	Mark 8:22-26	John 4:46-54
Matthew 15:29-31	Mark 9:1-10	John 5:1-15
Matthew 15:32-39	Luke 4:31-37	John 9:1-12
Matthew 17:1-9	Luke 4:38-39	John 11:38-44
Matthew 17:14-21	Luke 4:40-41	
Matthew 20:29-34	Luke 5:12-16	

What is the warning in these verses?

Matthew 7:15-23	Matthew 12:31-32	Acts 5:1-11
Matthew 12:22-30	Mark 3:28-30	
Mark 3:20-27	Matthew 13:53-58	

What did Jesus command us to do?

Matthew 28:16-20	John 4:23-24	Mark 8:34-38
Luke 11:9-13	Matthew 16:18-19	Mark 16:14-18
John 3:3-8	Matthew 16:24-27	Romans 8:1-11

What is the promise and purpose of the Holy Spirit?

Luke 24:46-49   John 14:23-26   John 20:19-22

John 7:37-39   John 15:26-27   Acts 1:1-8

John 14:12-21   John 16:5-15

What happened during the first outpouring of the Holy Spirit in the upper room on the Day of Pentecost?

Acts 1:12-15   Acts 2:1-13   Acts 2:14-47

How did the Holy Spirit manifest Himself and empower the disciples for their ministry?

Matthew 10:1-8	Acts 8:26-40	Acts 14:21-28
Acts 3:1-10	Acts 9:1-30	Acts 16:5
Acts 3:11-26	Acts 9:31	Acts 16:6-10
Acts 4:1-22	Acts 9:32-43	Acts 16:16-24
Acts 4:29-31	Acts 10:1-48	Acts 16:25-34
Acts 4:32-37	Acts 11:1-18	Acts 18:1-17
Acts 5:12-16	Acts 11:19-26	Acts 18:22-23
Acts 5:17-32	Acts 12:1-24	Acts 18:24-28
Acts 5:40-42	Acts 13:1-12	Acts 19:1-10
Acts 6:1-7	Acts 13:42-52	Acts 19:11-20
Acts 6:8-15	Acts 14:1-7	Acts 20:7-12
Acts 7:51-60	Acts 14:8-18	Acts 20:17-38
Acts 8:4-25	Acts 14:19-20	Acts chapters 21- 28

What do these verses tell us about the work of the Holy Spirit in our lives today?

Romans 5:1-5	Romans 15:15-21	2 Corinthians 3:17-18
Romans 7:5-6	1 Corinthians 2:1-5	Galatians 5:16-26
Romans 8:1-11	1 Corinthians 2:6-16	Galatians 6:7-10
Romans 8:12-17	1 Corinthians 3:11-17	Ephesians 4:25-32
Romans 8:26-28	1 Corinthians 6:9-11	1 Thessalonians 5:19-20
Romans 14:16-17	1 Corinthians 6:12-20	1 Peter 4:14
Romans 15:13	2 Corinthians 3:1-8	2 Peter 1:16-21

What are our instructions regarding the gifts of the Spirit?

1 Corinthians 12:1-11	1 Corinthians chapter 13	1 John 4:1-3
1 Corinthians 12:12-31	1 Corinthians chapter 14	

Ten Questions for Personal Reflection and Goal Setting

1. Have you received the baptism of the Holy Spirit? How often do you pray in your prayer language? Do you need a refilling of the baptism of the Holy Spirit?

2. Has God given you one or more gifts of the Spirit? How have you used them to honor and bring glory to God?

3. For the next two weeks, keep a time log of the things you do from morning until night. At the end of two weeks, look at the time you spent on various activities. What will you sacrifice to spend more time in the presence of the Lord?

4. What spiritual disciplines (prayer, fasting, Bible reading) are you lacking? How often do you engage in these activities?

5. Have you read the Bible from Genesis to Revelation? Set a personal goal to read the entire Bible in one year. Decide on the best location and time of day for reading. Discipline yourself to do this each day.

6. How often do you fast? Do you wait until you are in the middle of a

spiritual battle? Or do you fast regularly, whether you need an answer from God or not? Set a goal to discipline yourself for regular fasting.

7. How much time do you spend in daily prayer and communion with the Lord? Have you established a regular schedule to spend time alone with God? What is the best time of day for you? What are you willing to sacrifice to have this time with the Lord?

8. Are there sins in your life that are keeping you from operating in the fullness of the Holy Spirit? How many obvious sins of the flesh (Galatians 5:19-21) do you need to confess and repent of? Do you have hidden and unrepentant sins in your life?

9. How many of the fruits of the Spirit (Galatians 5:22-23) do you have in your life? Which ones do you still need to work on?

10. How many people have you led to Christ in the past year? What can you do to become a more effective disciple of Christ?

Photo Gallery

A. Fred Stone (left) with Lloyd Addair. Both had just been called to preach.

B. (left to right) Fred's father, William, Fred, and his half-brother Morgan

C. Fred and Juanita's wedding, July 1955

D. Fred and Juanita met in November, 1954

E. Aftermath of the car accident in 1961 that could have taken our lives.

F. Diana was healed at age 4

G. Fred with his parents, Bill and Nalva

H. The Bava family at Blackwater Falls, WV. (John, Lucy, Janet, Juanita)

I. A healing at Frankie Powell's church in Oneonta, AL

J. Fred and Juanita's 50th Wedding Anniversary, July 2005

K. Fred and Juanita with children and grandchildren, 50th Wedding Anniversary

Notes: